on evolutionary anthropology

an anthropological series

edited by jacques maquet

other realities

volume seven

undena publications
malibu 1986

on evolutionary anthropology
essays in honor
of
harry hoijer
1983

by

l. l. cavalli-sforza
h. harpending and p. draper
s. m. stanley

b. j. williams,
editor

published for
the ucla department of anthropology
by
undena publications
malibu 1986

Library of Congress Card Number: 85-52127

ISBN: 0-89003-170-3, cloth; 0-89003-171-1, paper.

© 1986 The Regents University of California

Undena Publications, P.O. Box 97, Malibu, CA 90265

CONTENTS

ISSUES IN BIOLOGICAL ANTHROPOLOGY

B.J. Williams

It appears that, in each decade, the practitioners of a discipline sit down and, in one forum or in many, identify and discuss the major issues of the discipline. The extent to which these issues can be agreed upon as the major issues can be regarded as a measure of how integral the discipline, as it stands in that decade. How rapidly these issues change is a measure of the progress of the field. Those issues which are so specific as to elicit little agreement that they are the major issues need not be surveyed in a broad forum. Those issues which are 'timeless' are, in another sense, those which are fruitless. In this slim volume we believe we have identified and dealt with issues in the middle range, having the characteristics that they are both broad enough to be of general interest as major issues and well enough defined to be profitable to consider, in other words, amenable to evidence and logic.

I believe that we can identify at least five such issues in biological anthropology upon which most can agree; they are in this exciting range of being both important and yielding to research. Three of these are dealt with by outstanding scholars well qualified to address each area. The first two issues concern the relationships between human biology and human culture. The first is, can biological or, specifically, genetic data aid us in understanding culture evolution? The second is this; is there genetic variation within populations, specifically, genetic polymorphisms, which influences cultural evolution or which need be accounted for in understanding human behavior patterns? The third question is more strictly biological and deals with the fossil record of human evolution; has the evolution of hominids been punctuational? And the fourth and fifth major issues, which we choose not to deal with in this volume are these: Is most protein evolution the result of selectively neutral substitutions among codons. And, how valid and how accurate is the molecular clock?

The latter two questions have excited much interest for the past 15 to 18 years, not just in anthropology but in all evolutionary studies. Both issues have enjoyed many reviews and presentations. This does not mean that they are resolved as issues. But it seems that they are close to being resolved. What is needed in each case is quite simply, more of the right kind of data. The only surprising thing is that, while neutralism and the molecular clock are closely related, they appear to be headed toward opposite fates. The molecular clock has received a great many confirmations and no refutations with data.

This does not mean that the presently dominant practice of calibrating the molecular clock, on a simple semilog plot of genetic distance against time, will be the final word, although it could be. It does mean that evolution of the total genome is some monotone function of time; it is clocklike. On the other hand, the accumulated data from DNA sequencing shows an overwhelmingly larger rate of substitution of third position nucleotides as compared to first or second position nucleotides. Since the third position nucleotides specify, mostly, synonymous codons, their rate of substitution is a rough measure of a neutral rate of substitution. This means that selection has, in general, strongly conserved first and second position codons; therefore has conserved amino acids. This is a falsification of expectations under the neutral hypothesis. The issue now may be that of reconciling the fall of neutralism and the success of the molecular clock. This may be resolved by comparisons of clocklike changes in the DNA itself with clocklike changes in proteins, especially over shorter time intervals. This, again, simply requires more data and will not be addressed in these pages.

A major set of issues in biological anthropology is concerned with the relationships between biology and culture. Stated at such a broad level this is one of the timeless problems, best ignored. But there are more specific issues of major importance within this overly broad set. One such issue is this: To what extent can we use the data of human biology and more specifically, genetic data to aid in our understanding of cultural evolution? We could make quite a different question of this by stating the preceding in reverse order: To what extent can we use data on cultural differences to aid in our understanding of biological evolution? But this later question is not a major issue. Evolutionists well accept the idea that, in order to study microevolutionary changes in populations, we need information on the breeding structure of those populations. Indeed, most in population genetics today subsume breeding structure under genetic structure for the purposes of studying biological evolution. In turn, the breeding structure of human populations is strongly influenced by the social organization and belief systems of that population. In addition to this we know that selective factors, rates of gene flow, the likelihood of survival of a mutation, and all other parameters characterizing the dynamics of evolutionary change, are profoundly alterable by cultural practices.

As we can see, the latter question, cultural influences on biological evolution, hardly exists as a general issue. It exists only in specifics. But, on the first question stated, can genetic data aid us in understanding cultural evolution, there is little agreement and great potential for acrimonious disagreement.

This potential for disagreement is rooted in the history of anthropology. Most uses of biological data in discussions of culture history, or conjectures on general cultural evolution in the 19th century and the early part of the 20th century, were based on serious confounding of what was cultural versus what was biological; or, what was genetic versus what was environmental, in human affairs. This provided a rich field for the expression of racism and other prejudicial biases between groups. One of the major

contributions, perhaps the major contribution of anthropology, was formulated at this time. This was the definition
and clarification of what was "cultural." This permitted, in
large measure although not entirely, the distinction between
what was cultural inheritance versus what was biological
inheritance. This was elaborated beginning with E.B. Tylor
and going through the work of Franz Boaz. But the reaction to racism, both scientific as well as lay, led eventually
to the more extreme Boasian position in anthropology. This
extreme position is that, not only are cultural and biological
change processes independent but, also, that we should not
consider biological data in any study of culture.

That this was a reaction to the racism of the day was
well documented by Freeman (1982). It was an extreme
reaction which was socially useful in the society of that day
but which went too far in many ways. Today that reaction
has moderated somewhat. Whether or not this moderation is
a result of progress in ameliorating injustices between
groups is arguable. Whether or not this moderation is a
result of changes in the attitudes of individuals is even
more arguable, given the surprising reactions to Freeman's
work (Brady 1983). But, clearly, there has been a change
toward a more balanced view, at least in terms of the
balance of people with different opinions within anthropology. In any event, more investigators feel confident that
they can return to these issues today, not as philosophical
or ethical issues, but as a practical concern in culture
history reconstruction. In so doing they may not only shed
light on specific culture history sequences but add to our
understanding of general processes.

L.L. Cavalli-Sforza addresses this issue in his chapter,
Diffusion of Culture and Genes. He shows that the distribution of blood group gene frequencies in eastern Europe fits
very well the idea that the spread of agriculture, specifically early Neolithic grain cultivation, from the Middle East
into Europe was a result of the movement of peoples far
more than the movement of ideas. In doing this Cavalli-
Sforza moves with data into an area where, before, there
had been only speculation. This represents an epidemio-
logical model for the spread of agriculture. Such models

have been a focus of concern for Cavalli-Sforza and co-workers for some time (Cavalli-Sforza and Feldman 1981). Ammerman and Cavalli-Sforza developed quantitative models for the rate of spread of agriculture into Europe, based on the archaeological record (Ammerman and Cavalli-Sforza 1971;1973). With gene frequency distributions Cavalli-Sforza is able to make a rather convincing argument that peoples, not just cultural adaptations, were displaced, to a large extent in this transition.

Migration theories are not unknown in anthropology. Indeed, they were rampant in anthropology from the beginning of the century to well into the 1950s. These were theories on the migration of peoples as a way of explaining prehistoric culture change, particularly technological change. These theories were never substantiated by evidence other than the evidence of culture change which they were to explain. This led, inevitably, to a strong reaction against migration theories in general. One of the longest running controversies over migrations has been called the "parallel phyla" hypothesis of paleolithic cultures. The parallel phyla hypothesis portrayed two major paleolithic tool traditions, the core tool tradition and the flake tool tradition. These two traditions were assumed to be carried by two different groups of humans. The distribution of the two tool traditions represented migrations and consequent distributions of these two groups of humans. This was never confirmed.

A similar hypothesis equated Neandertal in an invariant way with Mousterian tools. Migrations, to be believable today, most have supporting evidence in biological markers, preferably markers that give gene frequencies. At how distant a point in time will migrations into an already populated area leave their mark on present day gene frequency distributions? Cavalli-Sforza presents a case which is earlier than most of us would have guessed.

To what extent can we use genetic data to aid in our understanding of cultural evolution? This is not one major issue but two. As noted in the preceding paragraphs, the contribution by Cavalli-Sforza deals with the utility of genetic data to shed light on specific culture history sequences and perhaps, in so doing, to elucidate more general processes. The second major issue can be stated as follows: Is there genetic polymorphism in the human species today which influences cultural evolution or which need be accounted for in understanding human behavior? This is far more controversial than the first issue. We must stress that the issue is polymorphism and human behavior, not polytypism. For those unfamiliar with this terminology the polymorphic/polytypic distinction is the same as the within-group/between-group distinction. Despite a growing interest in behavioral genetics we are in little better position to analyse between-group genetic effects on behaviors, if such exist, than we were at the beginning of this century. It is not the models for analyzing such traits as behavioral traits do not exist; it is, quite simply, that they can be carried out successfully only under experimental controls of a rigor that make them inapplicable to human populations.

Such a stricture does not apply to the analysis of within group differences, to polymorphisms, which may be important. In comparison to other species there are still great limitations on what can be done in the genetics of quantitative traits (of which behavioral traits are a subcategory) of humans. But humans are, by far, the more interesting species. What are the possibilities in this area?

This brings us to the second major issue we confront in this volume, in the contribution of Henry Harpending and Patricia Draper in their chapter, Selection Against Human Family Organization. This article is intended as a challenge; and it is also a reply to a challenge. Those who deal with models for the genetic evolution of social constraints among humans have been challenged to produce evidence from data on humans, not just data on insects. Can we do better than post hoc explanation or 'illustrations' of a point? Harpending and Draper face this directly and provide a challenging example.

Here is a setting in which to consider this important contribution by Harpending and Draper. The concept of equilibria states is quite important in population biology. They are frequently studied in population genetics and in population ecology. Some of the more interesting equilibria studied are 'frequency dependent' equilibria. One such frequency dependent equilibrium state, which has fascinated naturalists since the mid-19th century, has to do with mimetic insects. Some insects contain chemicals which make them highly unpalatable to the birds which would otherwise devour them but for their offensive taste. Birds must learn that such insects are distasteful, so this does not protect every individual insect of the species. But it works fairly well. Other insect species are often found which mimic the unpalatable species, either in behavior, coloration, form, or in all three characteristics. The mimetic species is well protected from predation also, as long as it is much rarer than the unpalatable species. This is the frequency dependent aspect of predator avoidance. If the mimic becomes more common, relative to the unpalatable species, the casually experimenting bird is rewarded frequently enough by the palatable species that predation increases on both. It can be shown that a frequency dependent equilibrium exists in this system.

Most of the models of behavioral ecology or sociobiology are also frequency dependent models. They are models of frequency dependent rates of evolution and/or frequency dependent equilibria states. One of the simplest and most widely known cases of this kind is Triver's (1971) conjecture on the evolution of cheating behavior among altruists. Much of social life involves cooperative behavior. A little of social life also involves altruistic behavior. In each case the behaviors are predicated, for the most part, on the expectation of reciprocity, either direct or indirect.

In any situation where cooperative behavior is displayed by almost all members of a society, but there is opportunity for advantage (fitness advantage is envisioned in the models developed in behavioral ecology or sociobiology) for the individual who fails to cooperate or otherwise play by the rules, then cheating behavior will evolve. But just as with the mimetic insect this advantage is frequency dependent. As the cheaters become more common they lose their advantage. This can occur, in some instances, because they have an advantage only when rare. In other instances it appears that there has been a coevolution of behaviors in the population to limit cheating.

These are general comments. What have they to do with prediction in human society? Humans are highly social animals. Human society, in all it's different manifestations, embodies the conditions under which the evolution of some cheating behaviors, having a genetic basis, would be predicted by Triver's hypothesis. Do such exist? Harpending and Draper believe they have found a major example of such a phenomenon in human society; a polymorphism in which the deviant group may account for as much as 10 percent of the population. If this holds up, our own species will constitute one of the major exemplars of this kind of behavioral evolution.

The third major issue addressed has nothing to do with culture. Steven Stanley, in his chapter, Is Human Evolution Punctuational? addresses a major problem, the mode of human evolution. It may not be completely accurate to say that this has nothing to do with human culture. In it's inception the theory or doctrine of punctuated equilibria represented either an analogy or a direct extension of the Marxist idea that human society changes in major ways only by revolution, not by slow and continuous evolution. This may be a slight bowdlerization of Marx's idea but that this was the origin of punctuated equilibria is not in doubt (Gould and Eldredge 1977). Regardless of it's origin, and regardless of whether it is analogy or not, the punctuational interpretation of fossil sequences stands or falls on it's own internal logic, and on evidence.

The punctuational mode of evolution is quite clearly drawn. It is not simply a descriptive term. It does not simply mean that evolution is not "straight line." There has been no one, for a long time, in paleontology, human or otherwise, who believes that rates of morphological evolution do not change. At times a trait will change rapidly, at times slowly. Punctuated equilibria is much more than this. It is a theory of evolution by speciation and species selection. It has the following characteristics:

1) Large species cannot evolve rapidly enough to produce changes seen in the fossil record. They evolve little or none ("stasis").

2) Rapid change ("punctuation") occurs at the time of speciation.

3) This change occurs as a result of gene drift in a small population; usually allopatric.

4) Speciation and associated changes are, therefore, geologically instantaneous.

5) The parent population does not change and usually becomes extinct.

6) Speciation is random with respect to fitness.

7) Long term trends in the fossils record are a result of species selection.

The first five characteristics were those elaborated by Eldredge (1971), Eldredge and Gould (1972), and Gould and Eldredge (1977). The final two criteria are the work of Steven Stanley, the contributor of this chapter. These two latter criteria are referred to as "species selection" but are considered by most workers to now be an integral and important part of the overall "punctuationalist" position.

The punctuationalist position is still far from universal acceptance among paleontologists, and its critics have been quick to point out apparent weaknesses (Charlesworth, Lande and Slatkin 1982; Levinton and Simon 1980; Schopf 1982; Templeton 1980). One of the strongest advocates of the punctuational position is Steven Stanley. He believes that the homind fossil record is one of the best cases of punctuational evolution and he develops that case in his chapter, Is Human Evolution Punctuational?

REFERENCES

Ammerman, A.J. and L.L. Cavalli-Sforza
1971 Measuring the rate of spread of early farming in Europe. *Man* 6:674-688.

1973 A population model for the diffusion of early farming in Europe. In *The Explanation of Culture Change*, ed. by C. Renfrew. London: G. Duckworth and Co., pp. 343-357.

Brady, Ivan, ed.
1983 Speaking in the name of the real: Freeman and Mead on Samoa. *American Anthropologist* 85:908-947.

Cavalli-Sforza, L.L. and M.W. Feldman
1981 *Cultural Transmission and Evolution: A Quantitative Approach.* Princeton, N.J.: Princeton University Press.

Charlesworth, Brian, Russell Lande, and Montgomery Slatkin
1982 A neo-darwinian commentary on macroevolution. *Evolution* 36:474-498.

Eldredge, N.
1971 The allopatric model and phylogeny in Paleozoic invertebrates. *Evolution* 25:156-167.

Eldredge, N. and S.J. Gould
1972 Punctuated equilibria: an alternative to phyletic gradualism. In *Models in Paleobiology*, ed. by T.J.M. Schopf. San Francisco: Freeman, pp. 82-115.

Gould, S.J. and N. Eldredge
1977 Punctuated equilibria: the tempo and mode of evolution reconsidered. *Paleobiology* 3:115-151.

Levinton, Jeffrey S. and Chris M. Simon
1980   A critique of the punctuated equilibria model and implications for the detection of speciation in the fossil record. *Sytematic Zoology* 29:130-142.

Schopf, Thomas J.M.
1982   A critical assessment of punctuated equilibria I. Duration of taxa. *Evolution* 36:1144-1157.

Templeton, Alan R.
1980   Macroevolution. *Evolution* 34:1224-1227.

DIFFUSION OF CULTURE AND GENES

Luigi L. Cavalli-Sforza

The geographic patterns of human cultures and gene pools show surprising similarities. In fact, the "cultural areas" defined by Murdock are very similar to those of the geographic distribution of major human "races." No attempt at classifying "human genetic areas" on the basis of distributions of gene frequencies has really been made, for the very good reason that there usually are no sharp discontinuities in the geographic distribution of genes. But a qualitative evaluation of maps of human genetic patterns obtained by multidimensional analysis of gene frequency data (Piazza et al. 1981) is in basic agreement with the most common classifications. In the last century, the idea that important cultural differences accompany human "racial" or physical differences took explicitly the form of "racism," essentially the belief in the genetic determination of behavioral differences between groups which led to the modern distribution of power and economic development among the nations of the world. Of course, it should be enough to consider in some detail the history of the geographic distribution of power to see how scientifically fragile this thesis is. Nevertheless, the correlation of the geography of culture and that of genes is a fact that can superficially lend credence to racism or, more generally, to the determination of cultural differences by genetic differences.

It is very well known that a correlation between x and y can in principle be explained by 1) x causing y, 2) y causing x, 3) both x and y being determined by one or more factors, or 4) a mixture of these hypotheses. It is easy to believe that extreme behavioral differences, such as those found between different species, are genetically determined, even in the absence of direct proof (which is usually lacking). But there remain great difficulties in proving that behavioral differences within the human species are genetically determined, and at the moment it is only for some extreme behavioral differences within the species that there is good evidence of genetic determination. It seems to me there is equally good evidence that the similarity of human genetic and cultural geographic patterns depends on the fact that they *both* depend in a coherent way on patterns of isolation and migration, which in their turn depend on geography, ecology and history.

The theme of this essay is to emphasize the main ingredients behind this correlation: 1) For sure, geographic and ecological conditions favoring local isolation or migration can serve as barriers or channels simultaneously for genes and ideas. However, the correlation between genes and culture would probably be far less dramatic than it is. 2) Certain groups of people are at some time in their history capable of great expansion, both in numbers and in space (much of this depending on specific technological advances). 3) Some cultural traits are highly conserved, so that people settling in new areas will retain much of their culture even for long periods of time. I will give two examples which may help illustrate these ideas.

The Neolithic Spread to Europe from the Middle East

My first example has to do with the spread of agriculture from its places of origin. There is agreement that most of the plants which were grown during early Neolithic in Europe (especially wheat and barley) did originate elsewhere, in Turkey and the Middle East, where their wild counterparts were first cultivated. Some archaeologists have indicated their belief that the spread of cultivation was *cultural* , i.e. , the new technology, including cultivated plants and animals was acquired by preexisting hunter/ gatherers through cultural contact with neighbors who had already converted from food collection to food production. The theory of cultural diffusion seems to have become fashionable as "migrationism" was falling into disrepute, probably because of the naivety of some previously popular migrationist interpretations. However, even recently other archaeologists have stated that at least part of the spread, for instance that of the "Bandkeramik" (linear pottery) was *demic* (due to displacement of people, i.e. of the farmers themselves). But the archaeological findings are usually uninformative on the point. It is rarely possible to say who inhabited the caves and huts, or used the artifacts found in archaeological surveys and excavations, so that there can be very little direct evidence on whether the spread of agriculture to Europe was cultural or demic, i.e. of farming or of farmers.

A first analysis of the problem asked whether the rate of spread was compatible with the idea of demic diffusion, which obviously must depend on constraints due to human displacement and population growth. An examination of the archaeological literature made it possible to put on a quantitative basis the rates of the spread of the neolithic to Europe (Ammerman and Cavalli-Sforza 1971, 1973, 1976, 1984). The basic data were the first arrivals of the neolithic in the best known archaeological areas of Europe, as witnessed by the cultivation of wheat and, in most of Europe, use of pottery. The results showed a linear relationship between distance from the "center" of origin (the "center" being the nuclear area where agriculture first developed in the Middle East) and the time of first arrival. This is tantamount to saying that the velocity of the spread was constant; it was also low (of the order of one kilometer per year). There were exceptions: the velocity was some what greater in the Mediterranean, where boats could be used, and in the plains of Germany and Poland, where streams were abundant and near which settlements took place; and it was slower where there were ecological obstacles (e.g. in Switzerland and Scandinavia).

This result is of course consistent with either theory of spread, demic or cultural. But the question arises: Can the observed rate of spread be maintained by the rate of growth of human populations, and their migration rates? Especially with the almost total absence of means of transportation migrations were of necessity slow. The archaeological record is practically silent on questions of instantaneous rates of population growth and migrations. Demographic data taken from the ethnographic records provide estimates of *potential* rates of demic spread which are in reasonable agreement with the observed 1 km./yr. Thus the demographic constraints of population growth and movement do not contradict the hypothesis that the spread of agriculture was one of farmers and not of farming only. One would of course like more direct evidence which, unfortunately, archaeology does not provide.

There is better hope to distinguish between demic and cultural diffusion, or to evaluate their relative role if both are responsible for the spread of agriculture to Europe by considering the gene pool of current European populations. One may reasonably fear, of course, that data on today's populations may hardly reflect events that occurred between 9000 and 6000 years ago. Many other population movements must have occurred since, including many that are historically known. Unfortunately, data available from the fossil record, in particular from bones, do not include traits clearly transmitted without influence from the environment; only data on genes are reasonably safe. In fact, environment can affect the frequencies of various alternatives of a gene (alleles) only by natural selection, usually a slow process. Furthermore, genes more sensitive to natural selection can often be identified and excluded from analysis. Except for such extreme cases, gene frequencies are highly conserved, i.e. are usually stable over time, and if data on enough genes are available, the comparison of gene frequencies in different populations can inform us about the remote origins and history of populations.

The information contained in all the genes for which there were enough data in Europe was summarized by calculating *principal components*, a statistical technique which allows one to weigh a multitude of variables so as to sort the major patterns present in the data, order them by importance, and display them graphically or otherwise. The leading principal component for a number of populations in Europe studied for 10 genes and 39 independent alleles gave a geographic map (Menozzi et al. 1978) which almost exactly paralleled the spread of farming from the Middle East, gradually mixing with preexisting hunter/gatherers of the local European populations, generated an almost circular cline of the genetic pool centered in the Middle East. Other alternative interpretations come to mind: First, natural selection caused by environmental changes (food, etc.) consequent upon agricultural practices may have affected gene frequencies so as to create the gradient observed. However, the fraction of the total variation in gene frequencies ascribed to the cline associated with the spread of agriculture is about 23%, and it is extremely unlikely that such a strong effect of selection can be observed in such a short time. Second, other migrations from the same area may also be responsible for the parallelism. The only one that comes to mind is that associated with the extension of *Homo sapiens sapiens* into Europe, which may have had a similar point of departure as that of agriculture. This however, should have happened some 34-40,000 years ago. Gradients of gene frequencies determined by demic expansion and not maintained by selection are unstable in time, because under the continuous genetic exchange going on between neighbors they fade and finally disappear. We have tested by simulation the stability of long clines of gene frequencies to later migration between neighbors. In these simulations, clines disappeared slowly, so that after the end of the spread of agriculture there would have been only a relatively small reduction of gradients, but they would almost entirely disappear after 40,000 years. Third, the clines are maintained by a selection gradient; but a circular cline of the type observed would demand very peculiar ecological conditions which have no similarity to the ecology of the region.

The principal components of order lower than the first also showed interesting patterns: the second indicated an east-west gradient, probably expressing migrations known to have taken place, in historical and prehistorical times, from C. Asia. The third principal component shows a maximum in Poland-Ukraine. It is interesting that this is the region from which, according to some linguists, the expansion of Indoeuropean-speaking people started about 5000 years ago. Thus, geographic maps of principal components offer the possibility of distinguishing patterns probably due to major past migrations, and rank them in order of the importance of their contribution to the gene pool differences.

We also tested by simulation the process of expansion, assuming that the population density of European hunter/ gatherers was low (in agreement with ethnographic estimates) and that it reached a density some 20x higher by early (neolithic) farming, an assumption in agreement with archeological and ethnographic observations. We gave 20 genes (with 2 alleles each) to the simulated local populations, and let them vary freely by random genetic drift prior to the expansion of farmers. "Farmers" were the local hunter/gatherers of the Middle East, and they were given the new growth potential (in practice, a saturation level of local logistic growth 20x higher than that of hunter/ gatherers) at a time corresponding to some 10,000 years ago; the expansion to Europe, at the observed rates of local migration, took about 4000 years. We also added, in the simulation, other migrations at different times and from different places, and could successfully resolve some of them by mapping principal components of the simulated gene frequencies (Rendine et al. 1983). The whole process was carried over for 10,000 years since the beginning of the expansion of agriculture.

The essential factors determining the gradient are: 1) the existence of genetic variation in the area covered by the expansion, prior to expansion; 2) the capacity of farmers to grow to a higher population density; 3) a relatively slow migration rate; and 4) the existence of some acculturation of hunter/gatherers. In order to see a gradient of gene frequencies similar to that actually observed, a certain amount of "acculturation" of local hunter/gatherers is necessary so that their genes can enter the gene pool of survivors after immigration of farmers. All the other assumptions that have to be made for simulating the process are less influential. The hypotheses made above seem all eminently acceptable. It is clear that a higher population density was reached under agriculture. It seems quite reasonable that the most important determinant in the present pattern of gene frequencies in European populations is the technological event which was responsible for the most important increase in population density. It is worth stressing that, for observing a genetic gradient such as the observed, the migration of farmers is not sufficient, but some absorption ("acculturation") of the local hunter/gatherers must take place, either by cross marriage or simple acceptance of the new technology. The rate of acculturation of local hunter/gatherers in contact with farmers in the simulations is, in fact, perhaps the most critical factor in determining the slope of the gradient of gene frequencies across Europe (Sgaramella-Zonta and L. Cavalli-Sforza 1973).

After 9-10,000 years of agriculture there are still hunter/gatherers in the world. They all live in marginal areas. This shows that the acculturation process is slow and cultural diffusion not as fast for certain activities, even for those which are as important as obtaining food. The switch to agriculture involves very deep changes in all customs. The acquisition of a wholly new pattern of life is demanding, and whenever conditions permitting the earlier pattern still exist, there will be considerable resistance to change. Even though human multiplication and migrations are slow, they may turn out to be faster, some times, than cultural adaptation of preexisting populations.

Parallel examples exist: The Bantu expansion from Nigeria to Central and South Africa is reasonably well documented (Hiernaux 1974; Bonquiaux 1980). If we extend our consideration to non-aboriginal populations, we find that with the improvement in transportation technology demic diffusion has taken even more massive proportions. After the fifteenth century, Europeans, under severe population pressure, practically replaced aboriginal populations of America and Australia. Again, population pressures plus new technologies were responsible for these expansions, and culture has accompanied genes (and helped their spread) so that both have expanded in a perfectly coordinated fashion. Similar demic events must have occurred a number of times since man became a truly cultural animal.

The Geographic Distribution of Cultural Traits

The second part of my presentation is superficially unrelated to the first. It summarizes unpublished research, generated by the desire to study some bona fide cases of cultural diffusion. Advantage was taken of the existence of the ethnographic atlas by Murdock, the well known survey of literature data which covers a great variety of anthropological traits in a number of traditional societies. Although it was called an atlas, there is no graphic presentation in Murdock's book; but it can be easily obtained by computer. Our analysis was started a long time ago, and has come to publication as a monograph only now (Matessi, Viganotti, and Cavalli-Sforza 1983). We confined our attention to Africa.

Figures 1 and 2 show examples of the geographic distribution of two of Murdock's traits, family organization and settlement patterns. Each trait is described in several modalities, listed in each figure and indicated by alphabet letters. The maps show the location and modality of each society that was studied. In case of overlap societies were moved to the nearest position available. The maps show that the societies studied are distributed very irregularly. There is a considerable concentration in some former English colonies, especially those more densely populated.

The distribution of the modalities of each trait show a degree of geographic clustering, as would be expected in the cultural spread of a modality around its place of origin. Naturally, the irregularity of the distribution of the societies for which data are available makes the analytic task more complex. Moreover, the displacements of tribes, which are numerous in African history as a consequence of

Figure 1

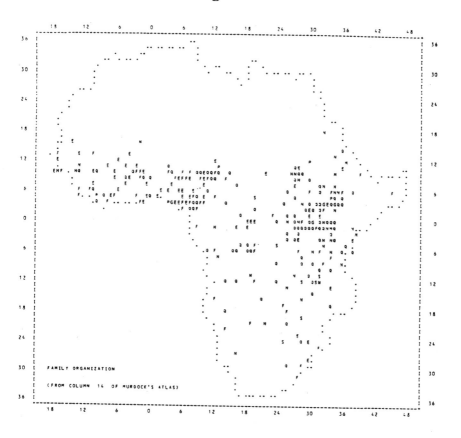

B   large extended families

F   small extended families

G   minimal extended families (only 2 related families, disregarding polygamy)

M   nuclear families, monogamous

N   nuclear families, only occasionally polygamous

P   polygamy (not sororal)

Q   as in P but cowives occupy separate quarters

R   polygamy preferentially sororal

S   polygamy same as R with cowives in separate quarters

　　　　　L.L. Cavalli-Sforza

Figure 2

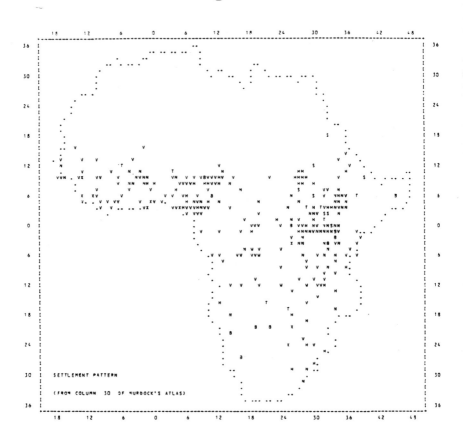

SETTLEMENT PATTERN

(FROM COLUMN 30 OF MURDOCK'S ATLAS)

B. Fully migratory or nomadic

H. Separate hamlets

N. Neighborhoods of dispersed family homesteads

S. Seminomadic (fixed settlement at some season)

T. Semisedentary (different fixed settlements at different seasons)

V. Compact and relatively permanent settlements

W. Compact but impermanent settlements

X. Nucleated village or town with outlying hamlets or homes.

tribal wars and of expansions like that of Bantu speaking people, must have contributed to complicate the present geographic distribution of cultural traits. In any case, all the maps we made are far from showing any clear-cut diffusion in circular waves, as might naively be expected by analogy to the "wave model" of linguistic diffusion. In other words, the cultural modalities of Murdock's atlas do not show isopleths as clear-cut as the "isoglosses" of dialectologists. The inspection of the maps reveals however a certain degree of geographic clustering, and the figures shown are selected among those that convey this visual impression more clearly.

We were interested in testing more accurately the degree of clustering of each modality of the various traits. To this aim, we tried various methods, mostly imitating similar ones used by ecologists to test the randomness of the geographic distribution of plants. A considerable methodological effort had to be made to modify existing methods for the specific purposes we had in mind. Different methods gave basically concordant responses, with discrepancies due to their different sensitivities, and their idiosyncratic behavior. The final conclusion was that almost all modalities of all traits are not randomly distributed in space. The methods chosen were mostly tuned to detect only the non-randomness due to *fine* clustering, that is to similarity between close neighbors, rather than non-randomness in the relative distribution of modalities among gross subdivisions of the whole continent, which are of lesser interest at this point. In other words, almost all modalities were geographically finely clustered. However, some factor, presumably the mobility of African societies, disturbs the regular patterns of diffusion that might otherwise be observed, and partially randomizes the geographic clusters, so that isopleths are difficult to visualize or construct.

There are, however, other factors to consider in trying to unravel the geography of cultural traits. One cannot exclude, a priori, the importance of demic diffusion for some of these cultural traits. Assume that, for some reason, a cultural trait is highly conserved i.e., it has a very low evolutionary rate because innovations are rare, or because they are not easily accepted. In the complex history of settlement of Africa, some groups have expanded much more than others, and inevitably split a number of times in tribes that have occupied different areas, split again, moved again, and so on. A highly conserved cultural trait will then spread with the people. Naturally there cannot have occurred only fissions, but also fusions, which will generate greater complexity; but with groups rapidly expanding in relatively unpopulated areas fissions are likely to have been more numerous than fusions. There is the possibility of building a relatively uncomplicated tree of demic descent, purely from genetic data, and testing if a conserved cultural trait spreads accordingly. Unfortunately, however, the existing genetic data are insufficient for reconstructing the history of differentiation of African tribes, a gigantic task given their numbers. They were enough, however, for Hiernaux (1974) to declare the substantial genetic homogeneity of Bantu speaking tribes. This, in the words I am using here, is equivalent to stating that the diffusion of Bantu languages was mostly demic.

With the exception just mentioned, the present gene pool data can be used only in a very limited fashion in Africa for reconstructing in any detail its demic history and comparing it with that of individual cultural traits to test if there was demic diffusion of these traits. But one can use another source of information, which is widely available and is probably the next best guide to demic history, linguistic data. Languages are highly conserved, and linguistic differentiation is highly correlated with genetic differentiation. Naturally there can be striking discrepancies. We know that in a few generations a language can be totally supplanted by a completely unrelated one. Hungarians show modest genetic differences from surrounding populations in the genetic map of Europe, although they speak a language unrelated to the Indoeuropean ones which are dominant in the rest of Europe. African Pygmies use Bantu and Nilotic languages which they certainly acquired relatively recently. But total replacement of a language by an unrelated one is relatively rare, being the consequence of political and historical accidents of considerable magnitude. Apart from these often easily traced anomalies linguistic similarities speak strongly for genetic affinities.

One can therefore correlate each cultural trait with the linguistic affiliation of each society, and thus obtain a test of the demicity of diffusion--with some cautions to be discussed later. Both cultural traits and languages are not simple quantitative, measurable traits, and the test for correlations can only be done by methods such as testing the randomness of contingency tables. Except for traits for which the modalities can be ranked, or traits existing each in two modalities only (i.e. with binary classifications) these correlations are difficult to measure with coefficients which express in a fully satisfactory way the strength of the associations. We have been content with testing the significance of the contingency tables formed by the modalities of the two traits being correlated. Because of the great number of correlations tested, we used a probability level (P=.001) that would make practically negligible the number of associations found significant by chance.

The results showed that the distributions of many cultural traits are indeed highly correlated with language distributions, giving prima facie evidence that demic diffusion may be involved for many of them. The characters correlated with language were not, however, spread uniformly among those listed by Murdock. The greatest number of correlations was found among characters of family and kinship. This finding has interesting interpretations; but before we go into them, we should consider another factor of importance. It is possible that some, perhaps many cultural traits represent adaptations to the physical environment. Unquestionably, subsistence strategies must be modified greatly, depending on the available fauna and flora, and technologies and materials with which houses are built must be tuned to the local environments. A study of the correlation with the physical environment has shown that precisely these traits are not randomly distributed with respect to the usual types of environment.

The results of these analyses are indicated in summary form in Table 1. The greater frequency of correlation of family and kinship traits with linguistic classifications

L.L. Cavalli-Sforza

compared with that for other types of traits is highly significant. By contrast, family and kinship traits are uncorrelated with environment. Some socioeconomic traits are correlated with language, some with ecology; the same is true of house building, while the category of "various" traits is correlated with neither. This group includes all characters related to sex (segregation of adolescent boys, insistence on virginity, sexual mutilation), religion and games.

Table 1

Correlations between Cultural Traits and Language or Ecology

Traits	Number of Traits	Correlations with	
		Language Group	Ecology
Family and kinship	13	10 (77%)	0 (0%)
Socioeconomic	16	7 (44%)	6 (37%)
House building	5	4 (80%)	3 (60%)
Various	6	0 (0%)	0 (0%)

Given in Table 1 are the number of traits correlating significantly (at P=.001) with language (3rd column) or with ecology (4th column) out of the total of traits tested (2nd column) or with ecology the corresponding percentages given in parentheses. Correlation is tested by contingency X^2. For instance, out of 23 traits related to family and kinship, 10 were correlated with language group, and none with type of environment.

It is also instructive to study the correlations between all traits (Table 2), but again, family and kinship and housebuilding show significantly more correlations among themselves than most other groups of traits. In part, this must be due to the fact that common demic descent will generate correlations between all traits that are correlated with it. But there are also likely to exist considerable internal constraints (for instance patrilineal or matrilineal descent are usually not confined to a single trait; authority and money tend to be passed on in the same way, and transmission of such traits will influence many others). The data are probably not sufficiently robust to try and disentangle correlation due to the common descent from that of reciprocal interaction between the traits.

Table 2

Correlations between Cultural Traits
Significance at P=1%

	Number of traits	Number of correlations signif/total	Proportion significance
Between traits affecting:			
Family and kinship (FK)	13	38/78	49%
Socioeconomic (SEP)	16	38/120	23%
House building (HB)	5	6/10	60%
Various (V: sex related, gods, games)	6	0/15	0%
Between FK and SE traits	13x16	12/208	6%
FK and HB "	13x5	9/65	14%
SE and HB "	16x6	19/80	24%
V and all others	6x34	0/204	0%

In summary then, family and kinship (and to some extent also housebuilding and some socioeconomic traits) seem to follow most closely demic history as evaluated by linguistic comparisons, and are not influenced by environment. Some other traits are also highly correlated with demic history, some with environment, some with both. The group of traits which we have labelled as "various" is least correlated with both; such traits are those for which it is most likely to find true cultural epidemics, i.e., the applicability of "wave theory." Not surprisingly, they are those for which the degree of geographic clustering (not given here) is high. The three models of clustering (demic diffusion, ecological adaptation, cultural diffusion or "wave theory" are presented schematically in Figure 3. Correlation with demic history (shown through that with languages) means that a trait tends to survive unchanged over generations in a population, in spite of its wanderings and, more importantly, of its fissions. This is the same as saying that it has a low rate of evolutionary change, i.e. is evolutionarily conserved. We therefore find this is a property characteristic of most family and kinship traits, housebuilding traits, and some socio-economic traits. (See Note p.33.)

There are also a number of other traits for which innovations can be adopted without constraints from other cultural characters or from the environment, and probably spread in an epidemic like fashion, i.e. in waves. The rate at which they spread, if it could be evaluated from historical information, would be indicative of rates of cultural contact, and of the acceptability of each innovation. In this geographic area however, diachronic information is usually lacking. Maybe clear (synchronic) isopleths could be constructed, say, for games, religions and other traits which seem to diffuse the cultural way, if more detailed categories than those employed by Murdock could be recorded. Maps for individual types of games, rather than the complex category "games of chance" or "games of skill" used by Murdock would be much more useful for purposes of cultural geography.

Figure 3

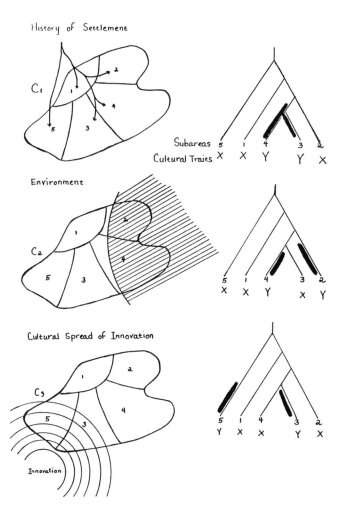

Lineages represent genetic descent of individual populations from common ancestral populations.

Family and Kinship as Highly Conserved Traits

The higher conservativeness of family and kinship characteristics is a clear-cut result which deserves further comment. In recent work with M. Feldman (1981) we have explored the long term evolutionary expectations of different modes of transmission of cultural traits. A simple consideration, that of the ratio of teachers to learners, permits one to predict the evolutionary effects of different transmission mechanisms, on the assumption that the mechanism remains the same over generations. Let us distinguish four possible mechanisms of culture transmission, noting that for most traits more than one mechanism may coexist, but one will usually be dominant. (Mathematical developments of evolutionary predictions for each of these mechanisms appear in the work with Feldman.)

1.   Parent-child (one-to-one, vertical).

2.   Social group pressure (many-to-one, or multiple oblique): the whole group, or many individuals who are socially closer to the learner (transmittee) act as teachers and usually do so in a coherent way, reinforcing each other's effects.

3.   Diffusion by one-to-one contact of individuals of the same generation (horizontal) or more generally, irrespective of age: This is the "infectious" or "epidemic" transmission.

4.   Teacher of social leader/to students or followers (one-to-many): This is characteristic of a society with schools, or with a political structure. In societies that do not recognize authority, or in which there is no organization of teaching other than on an individual (one-to-one) basis, this type of transmission must be limited. Where there are no power scales, or variation of wealth, only prestige can be a basis for imitation of one individual by many others.

These four mechanisms have entirely different evolutionary consequences. The first is analogous to biological transmission, and as such is highly conservative. Individual differences are conserved, innovation is possible but under selective control (both by natural and cultural selection), and populations will change at a rate similar to that of biological change, i.e. slowly.

In the second (many-to-one), conservation is even higher, but individual variation will tend to be reduced. Conformity (low individual variation) will be the result, and innovations have the least chance of acceptance. The extent to which individual variation is reduced and innovation discouraged depends on the power (pressure) exercised by the group of transmitters.

Horizontal transmission (mechanism 3) can bring about rapid change, but always, as in an epidemic, with a logistic-like type of increase among individuals of a population. It will lead to conformity only when the epidemic process goes to completion. Group to group extension will depend on the cultural contacts between the groups.

One-to-many transmission is the fastest mechanism of cultural change. Uniformity of the group is the final result and is obtained very rapidly, but innovations are possible and also spread rapidly. Group to group variation can be high.

It is clear that family and kinship principles are taught in the family, by the one-to-one mechanism and also by social pressure, at least within the family (and often at a wider level). Thus traits of this kind are expected to be highly conservative. A further consideration is that social norms taught in the family are of greater stability, during the life of an individual, because they are taught early, at a time when individuals are more plastic. Thus it is not surprising that norms concerning family and kinship show less change over generations, and are perhaps evolutionarily as stable as language, with which they will therefore show important correlations.

In the book with Feldman briefly summarized in the last few paragraphs, we have discussed cultural evolution more at the level of individuals than of groups, but it is clear that the characters studied by Murdock were recorded at the level of groups. Not all groups are homogeneous, however, and Murdock gives some information for characters that vary within a population. We have not used this information because it is too qualitative and fragmentary for our purposes. It is clear however that groups are not necessarily homogeneous. Most characters vary at the individual level, and are so transmitted. The spread from group to group of such characters is usually mediated by the contacts between single individuals of the two groups. And finally, for a first approximation, single groups can be considered of a type corresponding to that of the majority of its individuals.

Homogeneity of individuals of a group is likely, in fact, to be much higher for cultural than for biological traits, since most mechanisms of cultural transmission--with the exception of parent-child transmission--tend to increase cultural homogeneity of the social group.

For characters for which the social group behaves by definition as a unit (political or social structure, for instance), it is of course also formally correct to consider the group as a unit. Even for these characters, however, transmission between groups (at least its first stage, generation of awareness) must be from individual to individual, belonging to different groups. Change of political control and rules may (and most often does) depend entirely on the activity of one influential individual, or of a smaller group within the particular society which acts in unison. Even for strictly social phenomena it would be deleterious to ignore that it is always the individual who is the actor.

Conclusions

The main conclusion is that some aspects of cultural history are strictly associated with a gene pool, and some more than others. This can generate a false impression that genes determine culture. There may be room left for this to happen, but in much subtler ways than in those which a hasty conclusion from the correlation of gene and culture would suggest. Genes and culture are correlated because they are co-transmitted; that is, people carry both with them. The vagaries of demographic expansions associated with new cultural developments, permitting rapid demographic increase of some groups, can only magnify the geographic variation of genes and culture while retaining their essential associations, i.e. their covariation. However, for those traits which are least conserved or more sensitive to environmental conditions, the association can break down or never appear.

NOTE

This paper was written while the manuscript by Guglielmino-Matessi et al. was still in a preliminary phase, and the P=.001 significance threshold was used. It was later decided to use the 1% level, which somewhat increases the reliability of conclusions, although it changes them only marginally.

REFERENCES

Ammerman, A.J. and L.L. Cavalli-Sforza
   1971   Measuring the rate of spread of early farming in Europe. *Man* 6:674-688.

   1973   A population model for the diffusion of early farming in Europe. In *The Explanation of Culture Change,* ed. by C. Renfrew, London: G. Duckworth and Co., pp. 343-357.

   1985   *The Neolithic Transition and the Genetics of Populations in Europe.* Princeton, N.J.: Princeton University Press. (In press)

Ammerman, A.J., L.L. Cavalli-Sforza, and
  D.K. Wagener
  1976   Toward the estimation of population growth in
          Old World prehistory. In *Demographic Anthropology:*
          Quantitative Approaches, ed. by E. Zubrow.
          Albuquerque: University of New Mexico Press.

Bouquiauz. L., ed.
  1980   *L'Expansion Bantoue.* Paris: Societe d'Etudes
          Linguistiques et Anthropologiques de France,
          Paris.

Cavalli-Sforza, L.L. and M.W. Feldman
  1981   *Cultural Transmission and Evolution: A Quantita-*
          tive Approach. Princeton: Princeton University
          Press.

Hiernaux, Jean
  1974   *The People of Africa.* New York: Charles Scribner's
          Sons.

Matessi, G.R., C. Viganotti and L.L. Cavalli-Sforza
  1983   Analysis of geographic clustering of cultural
          traits. Ms. in preparation.

Menozzi, P., A. Piazza, and L.L. Cavalli-Sforza
  1978   Synthetic maps of human gene frequencies in
          Europeans. *Science* 201:786-792.

Murdock, G.P.
  1967   *Ethnographic Atlas.*   Pittsburgh. University of
          Pittsburgh Press.

Piazza, A., P. Menozzi, and L.L. Cavalli-Sforza
  1981   Synthetic gene frequency maps of man and selective
          effects of climate. *Proc. Nat. Acad. Sci., U.S.A.*
          78:2638-2642.

Rendine, S., A. Piazza, and L.L. Cavalli-Sforza
  1983   Simulation of the spread of early farming. Ms. in
          preparation.

Sgaramella-Zonta, L. and L.L. Cavalli-Sforza
  1973   A method of the detection of a demic cline. In
          Genetic Structure of Population, ed. by N.E.
          Morton. Honolulu: University of Hawaii Press.

SELECTION AGAINST HUMAN FAMILY ORGANIZATION

Henry Harpending and Patricia Draper

A decade or so ago most of the study of evolution was the study of adaptation. A major focus was how organisms were designed to function in their environment. Sexual selection was mentioned in the texts, but we didn't understand the profound differences between sexual selection and the kinds of selection imposed by an environment which doesn't fight back. Since then the pendulum is on the other side, and nothing seems so dull today as studies of the fit between organism and environment. In anthropology it seemed reasonable that sexual dimorphism in Man was related to throwing spears, while today that seems silly, and we are sure that dimorphism reflects struggles between males for access to females. Pendulums swing both ways, and we must be aware that lots of today's cutting edge theory will sound absurd in a few years. In this paper we will discuss some ways in which contemporary evolutionary biology enlightens aspects of comparative human domestic organization. Since this is a topic with a hefty load of personal, political, and moral overtones, we want to emphasize, at the beginning of the paper, the disinterested, tentative, and transient nature of scientific understanding. Following that, our central theme is that domestic organizations in human societies are diverse and complex and that this diversity has generated a corresponding diversity of mating strategies. According to present evidence, there are some of these which are genetically transmitted and some which are culturally transmitted. Ecological pressures may often favor nuclear families and high parental investment while social selection may favor other strategies.

Ground Rules

The essence of science is the development of a model which mimics things that happen in the world. The model is judged by its ability to predict things which were not already accounted for by some simpler model. This is the point of view given in any introductory textbook in the sciences, it seems obvious in that context, but it is not so obvious in Anthropology. Very few of us have any emotional investment in or strong political opinions about, say, mechanisms of gene regulation, which is why it is easy to follow the dispassionate course of elaborating models in the hard sciences. It is much more difficult to do the same thing about parenting, or love, or murder, because we have such strong and overriding feelings and convictions about such things.

If we were to tell an astronomer that we thought that the concept of phlogiston had outlived its usefulness as a scientific construct, he would probably agree. If we said energy rather than phlogiston, our astronomer would laugh at us. When we suggest to colleagues that culture is not yet a useful scientific construct, a few laugh, a few agree, but lots of them actually become upset. In the human sciences we have an emotional investment in our subject matter, and it interferes with the kind of disinterested crossword-puzzle approach to things done in the hard sciences.

Our strategy here is to pretend that we are scientists from some other planet, that we are looking at living things and evaluating the theory of evolution as a framework for understanding their behavior, and that we don't know that humans are anything special. Of course we don't believe that humans are nothing special, but we self-consciously try to divorce our feelings from our scientific understanding.

Theory can be irrelevant, but barring logical error it is not wrong. The reason that evolutionary theory is spreading so rapidly in anthropology is that it is consistent, coherent, and firmly linked with the rest of science. This is worth something. It seems to us that what is necessary right now is more elaboration and development of a general theory of human evolution, and not so much "hypothesis testing." Good theory is, after all, better than the data in many cases. Given this perspective, there are several consequences which we should make very explicit before we get down to business.

1. We are primarily concerned with models, because anthropology, unlike biology and the hard sciences, suffers from a lack of high quality theory. Things are complex enough that it is not always clear how to evaluate a model, so consistency and simplicity will be primary criteria for evaluating what we accomplish. Facts are not always what they seem. There has been for years a theory in biology that a Y-chromosome in a mammal makes it a male. This was such a clear notion that a few exceptions, people who were males but who had two X-chromosomes and no Y, were insufficient to generate any serious doubts about the theory. It later turned out that these people had fragments of a Y-chromosome attached to one of their X's (Gordon and Ruddle 1981). The theory was indeed better than the facts. Facts in anthropology are especially ephemeral.

2. In our opinion neither our data nor our theories are good enough for the kind of formalized hypothesis testing which we all learned in introductory statistics courses. There is a kind of veneer of scientificality which comes with all that, but it can be very misleading. For example every year a student or two decides to test current theoretical ideas by doing a cross-cultural tabulation. There are readily available coded data for a great diversity of subjects, and it seems like a natural arena for evaluating theory. One might examine the relationship, for example, between "matrilineal inheritance" and "pre-marital sexual behavior." It doesn't matter how this one goes; most of them show very weak or else no relationship at all. Is the theory bad?

Most of us know absolutely nothing about the pre-marital sexual behavior of our neighbors, our friends, and even our own children. We certainly don't know much about such things among the people where we do field-work. The data are noise. They reflect what people tell ethnographers, which is interesting and useful as information, but they don't necessarily say much about what people actually do. One of us, Harpending has looked at genetic markers in !Kung Bushmen families of the northwest Kalahari, and it is apparent that there is very little paternity error. Social fatherhood and biological fatherhood are very much the same. On the other hand Bushmen speak of lots of sexual dalliance (Shostak 1976). These are both useful but very different data about !Kung reproduction. A good theory could explain both why !Kung have such low paternity error and why they will confess to all sorts of romantic excess.

3. Theory is simple and stereotypical. This is unlike a lot of anthropology, where there is a premium on good writing and crafted narrative. Anthropology has many roots in the humanities, and the tradition of anthropology as literature is valuable. It is also fundamentally different from the scientific tradition. That the world is complex and convoluted is self-evident. Science gnaws away at the complexity but does not try to embrace it. Our modest aim is to find an explanatory structure which predicts some fraction of human behavior. We will try to sketch our ideas of part of such a structure: the point is that we are really describing a structure and not describing the real world, so that we will leave out the hedging and qualification appropriate to ethnographic description.

4. We should be very suspicious of language in any context, not just in ethnography. It is inconceivable that evolution could create an intelligent social creature that was routinely honest with conspecifics (unless it was a dedicated sterile altruist like a worker bee). An honest creature would always be foxed by those a little less honest and would lose fitness. Language certainly did not evolve entirely because it facilitated the communication of truth; it was helped along because it facilitated the communication of lies, or at least it helped hide the truth. The reason that scientists use mathematics is that they can communicate meaning with equations in a way that is almost impossible with words. In classical mechanics, for example, mass is

force multiplied by acceleration. That is, without ambiguity, its definition. A narrative definition of mass would be a semantic nightmare.

Lee Robins (1978) provides a short but excellent summary of the semantic dilemna in behavioral science. She is discussing sociopaths, who (we will claim below) are just like the rest of us only more so. Some psychiatrists have defined sociopathy to be the "inability to love" or the "inability to feel guilt." These are apt descriptions of the behavior of sociopaths. On the other hand, sociopaths can provide eloquent accounts of the terrible guilt or the great love that they feel. The question Robins addresses is whether they "really" feel guilt and love or are just pretending. Her conclusion is that it doesn't matter, since we can't know the answer. We should look at their behavior and not what they say about it. Allen Johnson (1978) describes other examples of differences between what happens in the world and what humans say about it.

These two domains, that of behavior and that of language, are hopelessly intertwined in many ethnographies. Most of us have done fieldwork bearing with us the implicit assumption that, except for mistakes, people tell us the truth and that this truth mirrors what they really do. We need to redo a lot of our field studies with this assumption out in the open to be tested.

The Machiavellian perspective that people may be liars until proven otherwise is helpful in understanding cross-sex antagonism and fear of women (Draper and Harpending 1982). In some groups men agree that women are dangerous and mysterious bearers of potentially great pollution. (Two excellent sources for obtaining a sense of these groups are Meggitt 1964; Murphy and Murphy 1974.) Men do elaborate things to protect themselves from things female, and they are pretty rough on women in some of these groups, while in others the women seem to have the men cowed (the difference may be in ethnographers rather than in cultures). What sense does this view of women make? It seems to contradict everything we think we understand about evolution and fitness. Males ought to like females.

This complex starts to make sense when it is regarded as a set of manipulative messages rather than as a description of how people behave. These are typically groups where there is a lot of face to face competition among males and little male work directed at feeding his own offspring. A male in such a group wants the other males to believe that women are dangerous and polluted. If he can convince them that it is true, then he will have access to females and increased fitness, while the others sit in the men's house, gossip, and argue. This sounds good, but the system can get him too. Having been told all his life about the dangers of women, he may start to believe it and act on it. The men may become snared in their own strategy trap. This perspective on male-female antagonism seems so obvious that it has to be correct, if only a partial explanation for the fear of women complex. It is a fine illustration of the way that we should interpret culture, at least when we have our scientist hats on. It has many interesting implications. We should suspect that all norms and values (until proven otherwise) are not really what their proponents believe and act on. They are what their proponents are trying to persuade everyone else to act on. Here is a glimpse of the real difficulty for evolution in designing a creature that depends on cultural transmission. He must be carefully designed so that he filters the appropriate from the inappropriate in what he learns.

Examples

The best way for us to get across what we take to be the spirit of scientific interpretation via simple models is to give several examples. These are not meant to be thorough accounts--they simply illustrate how the evolutionist's cold eye might help us understand (read predict) things which are otherwise puzzling.

We have all been depressed at one time or another. It doesn't feel very good. In fact we are so impressed with how it feels to be depressed that those feelings are our definition of what depression is. What happens when we liberate ourselves from feelings, put on the scientist's hat, and examine depression?

In the metric of fitness it just doesn't matter whether or not some one feels good or bad. A disinterested biologist who saw people lazing around, using very little energy, and not eating very much would interpret the behavior he saw in adaptationist terms, because the evolutionary paradigm imposes that kind of understanding of the world. He would say that they were just conserving energy. But energy conservation poses a real strategic problem: since people, unlike hibernating rodents, can't get their basal metabolic rate down very low, the inactive state is dangerous. A human continues to consume calories, even though the rate of consumption is less than it is when active. Eventually the energy-conserver must come out of it and actively seek food or else he will die. Feeling bad when we are depressed may just be the mechanism making it easy for us (most of us) to leave the inactive state.

This theory of depression leads to some (perhaps) testable predictions. A human should be depressed in the face of scarce resources when activity will not yield a net positive return.

We say that the theory is only perhaps testable because things like scarcity and expected return are filtered through the system humans use to perceive their environment and many of the interesting differences among us seem to be in our perceptual systems. The theory tells us why bereavement (=perceived massive resource loss) and inactivity (=perceived low payoff to work) should lead to depression. It also predicts that people whose ancestry was in very seasonal climates should be more prone to depression (i.e. find it easier to learn) than people with genes from non-seasonal environments. It just doesn't pay to be active in Sweden in February. We are not prepared to defend this theory of depression, although there are some chemical and behavioral similarities between depression in humans and hibernation in other mammals (Feierman, nd). There are surely many disorders and mechanisms which get lumped together under the one label of depression. We are using it just to illustrate how our feelings interfere with scientific reasoning and how explicity ignoring our own feelings and intuition may improve our insight.

Child abuse and neglect are another set of topics where our personal feelings and evolutionary logic separate (Korbin 1981). Most of our acquaintances are very strongly bonded to their children and the very idea of child neglect makes us disturbed and angry. With our biologist's hat on, we know that we are "playing a high parental investment strategy." Someone who neglects his children is, by this way of thinking, playing a different strategy. It is worth exploring this, even though we shall continue to think (personally) that most child abusers and neglectors belong in jail.

Figure 1 is a graph of the probability that a child reaches adulthood as a function of the child's age. The particular numbers given pertain to males on the island of Taiwan in 1910 (Preston et al. 1972:700) but we are interested in a principle and not on details. These Taiwanese figures represent high mortality levels by present world standards for national populations, but they are perhaps moderate to favorable by comparison with many tribal level peoples. The curve shows that a newborn baby boy has a probability of .53, slightly greater than one-half, of living to adulthood at age 20. If he reaches the age of 1, then his probability of living to 20 has increased to .72, while at age 5 it is .85. The survivors curve reaches one at age 20, the somewhat arbitrary standard we have taken to be adulthood. (Of course adulthood is a nebulous concept. It means something like the age when parental care is terminated, which in turn depends very much upon the subsistence system.) The dotted line on the same figure is entirely hypothetical. It is a guess of the probability of the child reaching adulthood if it is abandoned by its parent(s). Below the age of 1 the probability is near zero, although this will depend again upon the local social organization. The curve rises steeply at the age of weaning, because after this the child is much more likely to be able to hang around with siblings, relatives, and friends and get enough food to keep alive. Like the curve from the real census, our hypothetical curve for abandoned children reaches 1 at age 20.

Figure 1

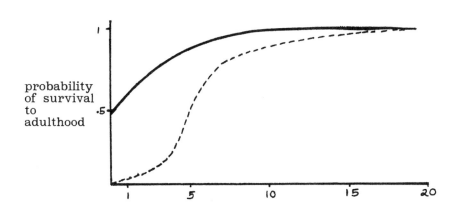

age of male child

This assumes that adulthood starts at age 20. The
solid line is census data for Taiwan males in 1920, the
dashed line is hypothetical survivorship with no
parental care.

These two curves are parameters for our model. Assuming that we are designed by natural selection to maximize
the production of adult offspring, and assuming further
that we have only two child-care options available, "invest"
and "abandon and start another", the question is straightforward: when, if at all, should we abandon our child?

We have to simplify the world in order to understand it at this point (see also Maynard Smith 1977). Let us say that I can abandon the child now, next year, the year after that, and so on. Each year I spend on the child in question costs me 1/8 of an adult offspring (this comes from assuming a birth spacing of four years and survivorship to adulthood and reproductive age of one half). Therefore if I abandon now I save time, while my expected loss is the difference between the child's probability of reaching adulthood with parental care and without it. The closer the two lines are in Figure 1, the less the cost of abandonment. For a newborn, the probability of survival to adulthood if abandoned is essentially zero unless someone adopts the child, while the probability of a nurtured child surviving is a little greater than one half. As the child grows up the two lines come together. When the distance between them shrinks to .125 (=1/8) the optimum parent will abandon the child and start another. This probably occurs soon after the child is weaned and can compete with the other kids for a share of the communal porridge pot.

This model is quick and dirty, but we are after qualitative insight from it, at least to start with. The gross predictions we get should be checked against the world. If they hold up, then we can think about sharpening it up. We know, for example, that parental investment can be graded. Fitness costs of time are different depending upon the growth rate of the population. There are any number of complications in modeling a process as complex as parenting. In general the enumeration of possible complications is not a very creative endeavor, so we will ignore them for the sake of clarity.

The most obvious gross prediction is that high fertility favors abandonment because the cost of time is higher. If fertility schedules were very high and mortality moderate then the cost of a year of investment in an older child might be one fourth of an adult offspring rather than one eighth. Second, high child mortality from care independent causes (like infectious diseases and accidents as opposed to malnutrition) favors abandonment because it diminishes the distance between the survivorship-with-care and survivorship-without-care lines. Low fertility, low child mortality levels, and isolated nuclear families (no communal pot nor children's peer group to forage with) favor longer investment. Is this heartless theory relevant to understanding what we see in the world? Perhaps not. Intensity and duration of child care and investment may be purely culturally transmitted, and we don't understand the mechanisms of cultural transmission as well as we do those of genetic transmission. It is certainly worth checking out, because there are a lot of children in this world who are not very well cared for. The prediction from evolutionary biology seems to be clear, even though our details could use sharpening: the kind of intense nurture which most of us practice is not necessarily that which has been favored by selection in most environments. From the perspective of a biologist from some other planet, the American middle class may practice aberrant child indulgence.

Many people in the world do not treat their children in the way that Americans think they should. In one ethnography after another of middle-level tribal societies there is a description of intense mother-infant contact and interaction until weaning, and outright maternal hostility and rejection afterward (e.g. LeVine and LeVine 1981; DuBois 1944; Kelekna 1981). Children typically eat with other children in these groups after weaning, often in outright scramble competition when food is scarce. The description of this pattern usually goes with assurances by the ethnographer that the child receives "emotional support" from peers and from others in the group. Our bet is that any of these kids would prefer a square meal to emotional support. The point here is that many people in the world do not share our American middle-class view that children need and deserve a lot of input. They treat children much as other primate parents treat their children, and they act in apparent conformity with predictions from evolutionary theory.

These two examples, depression and child neglect, should illustrate the way we think we should try to use evolutionary theory in our discipline. We want to emphasize that we advocate browsing in such fields as psychiatry, cross-cultural psychology, and others in order to try out theory. We don't really think that we have, now, very much to offer in return. It doesn't help someone with depression, for example, to be told that his affliction may be an adaptation. He still feels awful and wants relief. Further, there are variations of human behavior where we can't see that any evolutionary explanation makes much sense. Schizophrenia is an example, as is homosexuality (see Feierman 1982).

Strategy Conflicts Between the Sexes

Given the above, let us review some theory about the relations between the sexes in mammals. This is a straightforward rehash of discussion in Trivers (1972) and chapter 9 of Dawkins (1976).

The important idea is that there are profound differences in the way that the two sexes are engineered, especially in mammals, and that these differences generate very different options and strategies for the sexes to use to reproduce themselves. The sexual dimorphism is especially clear-cut for mammals.

Mammals are named for mammary glands, which are part of the complex of traits which define them--placentation, prolonged and intense parental care, prolonged immaturity, and the general "K-strategy" of making a high quality relatively durable product at the expense of a lot of input and care from the parents. But notice that most of these traits are in fact traits of females; males do not bear young, they don't even lactate. Given this, a male in trying to reproduce can play any mix, combination, or compromise of putting his reproductive effort into mating or into parenting--that is into being a cad or being a dad. Females have a choice too, although it seems somewhat more restricted than that of males. On the one hand a female can selectively find a mate who will provision her before she undertakes to reproduce--the feeder strategy--or she can ignore and forswear male provisioning and manage her own resource acquisition and apportionment--the breeder strategy. Many mammals and most humans do not exhibit any pure strategy. We are opportunistic, and our strategies change with age, resources, and opportunities.

Figure 2
Male Strategy Spectrum

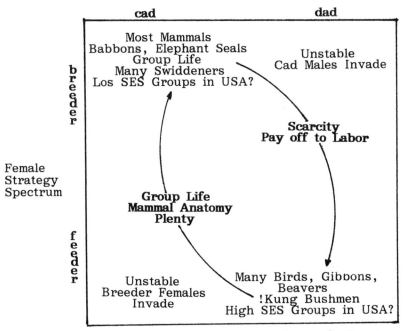

Model of reproductive Strategy options of the two sexes. See Dawkins 1976, Chapter 9

We assume that everyone is familiar with the Williams/ Trivers model of reproductive strategy, and we will say no more about it here. It is diagrammed in Figure 2. These ideas have gone from being outrageous to being trite in the space of about three to five years. Anyone who wants more should certainly read chapter 9 of Dawkins (1976) as well as all of Daly and Wilson (1983), where the comparative biology of reproductive strategy in animals is laid out in great detail. There is one idea implicit in this table which deserves more discussion here. When organisms compete with each other for something scarce, whether a food source or a mate, it should be very generally true that organisms most similiar to each other inflict the most damage upon each other. Thus if there are apple and cherry trees in an orchard, a bird committed to eating cherries and not apples suffers impaired fitness in proportion to the number of other cherry eaters, but no impairment from apple eaters. Such a situation often leads, in theory, to a stable frequency-dependent polymorphism. This means that when a type is advantaged when rare and disadvantaged when common, then a mixture of types should persist to comprise the population. The example here is dietary, but the best known example is Maynard Smith's (1976) model of hawk and dove strategists. In his model two hawks who meet have a vicious fight and one suffers great damage. A hawk always beats a dove--the dove just runs away. Doves have a mild fight when they meet, one wins at random, and the other loses. In this model, hawks get all the resources when they are rare, but as they become common they run into each other, inflict great damage, and lose their fitness advantage. A mix of both types persists (though the proportions fluctuate cyclically through time). Lewontin (1974) emphasizes the potential for frequency dependent polymorphisms to occur in genetic systems, and Maynard Smith (1982) has studied implications of the idea for social evolution in some detail. He calls the equilibrium mixture of types an ESS or "Evolutionary Stable Strategy." The general principle is vitally important for understanding the maintenance of diversity in social systems, in our opinion, as well as in genetics.

Transmission of Human Mating Strategy

The central point of this paper is that the diversity of human mating systems has led to polymorphism in mating strategy and, further, that looking at human mating strategies is informative about our own social evolution. We will discuss one trait complex which is transmitted predominantly through genetic material and one which is culturally transmitted. First, we will suggest that the complex of sociopathy and hysteria is a genetically transmitted social and reproductive strategy. These traits are usually treated as forms of mental illness in the literature, although as we point out below there are grounds to doubt that the medical model is appropriate. Although the perfect study has not been done, the evidence so far points without serious equivocation to genetic transmission of these traits with little if any cultural effect. This surprises us.

Following the discussion of sociopathy, we will review literature about the effects of father-absent child rearing. These effects are consistently described in the literature, and they are of interest because they make little sense in the context of naive and simple learning theory. We will argue that they make lots of sense, on the other hand, in the context of evolved learning propensities which, in the past, have maximized fitness. Father-absent rearing seems to lead to males and females with interests and abilities appropriate to reproduction in the context of competition with other males in the case of males and the context of reproducing fast and early without obtaining long-term male parental investment in the case of females.

Sociopathy and Hysteria

We all know that our complex web of expectations, obligations, and reciprocity is the major difference between human societies and those of other species. The thousands of implied contracts which we bear--from stopping at red lights to feeding our children--are absolutely qualitatively different from those of any known animal. Birdsell (1968) has described a "magic number" of 500 for dialect groups in various low energy societies. This seems to represent a capacity of our nervous system for knowing and remembering other people, and it is a huge number. This is all familiar to anyone in anthropology. We are going over it because the rich network of goods and obligations is tailor-made for cheaters to exploit. Modern evolutionary theory, the "Selfish Gene" and all that it implies, predicts that any complex social interaction will be an opportunity for cheaters and that, given enough time for the appropriate mutations to appear, they will invade, or at least "try."

As anthropologists we should know a lot about human society. If we were to design a cheater, how would we do it? What characteristics should a cheater have in order to take advantage of others in order to make copies of his (or her) own genetic material. Let us answer this from two viewpoints, first from the viewpoint of the flow of resources and how it might be siphoned, and second from the viewpoint of cheating on the system of parental care and pair maintenance.

Certainly our cheater would appear to be charming, open, and sensitive to others. We wouldn't design a hail-fellow-well-met, because that would be too obvious, but we would make an attractive, honest, and friendly phenotype. We would put no conscience at all into him, because conscience or ethics would simply interfere with his strategy. We would also make him invulnerable to the glues of friendship and trust. Since he would do very well until people discovered the way he was really designed, we would make him move all the time. The longer he stayed in one place, the worse he would do since people would discover his strategy. In the same way, we would put him in the anonymous environment of a big city where he could hide, rather than in a rural area with lots of face to face sociality. He would perhaps work in the way that others worked for a living, but he would also steal, cheat, and coerce whenever the opportunity arose.

He might marry, but he would not be a reliable provider of resources for his nest. He would abandon his family whenever an opportunity for something else arose, and he would also try to impregnate any other females possible. He should be especially good at convincing females of his ability to provide resources and to be a stable mate. In fact he should indulge in a determined promiscuity as he plays the basic mammalian cad strategy.

What if we were designing a female rather than a male? With respect to contracts and resources she should be much like the male. With respect to mating she should be adept at exaggerating her need and at extracting resources from males. She might copulate quite without choice in return for male investment, but she would not engage in long-term social contracts whether economic or reproductive.

What we would design, in fact, is exactly what psychiatrists call sociopathy and hysteria (Robins 1966; Guze et al. 1969; Robins and O'Neal 1958; Hare and Schalling 1978; Mednick and Christiansen 1977; Cloninger 1978; Goodwin and Guze 1979). It is known that these "disorders" are genetically transmitted (Bohman 1978; Cantwell 1975; Cloninger et al. 1975a, 1975b, 1978; Mednick and Hutchings 1978; Goodwin and Guze 1979), and the same genes which lead a male bearer to be a sociopath cause a female to be a hysteric.

Sociopathy goes by various names in the literature--psychopathy, antisocial personality, moral insanity are a few. The rigorous diagnostic criteria for the disease are pretty arbitrary and they don't make much scientific sense. We think that being a sociopath is like being tall. Everyone is a little bit tall, some more than others, and you only get called tall if you are near the tail of the distribution of height.

Most of the literature accepts this underlying quantitative model of sociopathy, at least implicitly, but we have a psychiatrist friend who says it isn't so. People are either cats or dogs, he says, and sociopaths are cats. The idea is that your dog really likes you, while if your cat were a bit bigger and you a bit smaller, your cat would happily eat you for supper. The appearance of a continuous underlying quantitative trait is just generated by more deceit, as if cats were trying to imitate dogs (Jay Feierman, personal communication).

Given these ambiguities, a sociopath is (usually) a male who has a life history of trouble with his parents, his community, and the law which started before adolescence. As a child he is a bad actor; he is called a "hyperactive child" these days. (Of course not all hyperactive children become sociopaths. One recent estimate is that approximately one third do, Wender and Klein 1981; see also Satterfield 1978; Mendelson et al. 1971; Brown 1979.) He is impulsive, unpredictable, and very active. He doesn't bond to other people very well, and interaction with him does in fact recall interaction with someone's cat (see the discussion of the limits to gullibility below). He is liable to be in trouble either for petty thievery or for "sexual misconduct" from a very early age.

As an adult he will have no close personal ties and he will not maintain the ties which he has, even with family. "My brother fits that pattern," a student told us the other day, "and we haven't heard from him in ten years." He is likely to be charming with an easy-going, open manner and a "facade of sensitivity" (Cloninger 1978). He won't hold a job for very long, and when he does change jobs it will be horizontally. He will be involved in illegal activities. Most crime is, in fact, committed by sociopaths (real crime, not parking tickets and not, perhaps, many crimes of passion). He will be a chronic liar, often for no good reason, and he will be very convincing.

His sex life is likely to be downright spectacular. The rates of venereal disease, illegitimate children, and broken marriages are very high among these people. He may have abandoned several females and offspring elsewhere, where he spent a year or so using different names.

He often has a mean temper, and a little bit of alcohol makes him act outrageous out of all proportion to the amount that he drank. He has an elevated risk of dying by violence or by accident, and his expectation of life is shorter than that of a non-sociopath.

He shows no signs of guilt, remorse, or anxiety. On the other hand he will sit down with a psychiatrist and report agonizing guilt, remorse, and anxiety. What do we make of this? Does he "really" feel these emotions or not? We can't know, and it doesn't matter very much. We are interested in what people do, not how they say that they feel (See Robins 1978).

The literature on sociopathy suffers from its medical origins. It is defined to be a disease, and careful objective diagnostic criteria are set up to classify people. If it really is a quantitative trait, then we want to study it as such, not as a category. Further, these people are criminals, especially when they are members of low socioeconomic classes. We believe that the same genes in the middle and upper class forge a person who shares many but not all of the book sociopath's traits. We all know people who may be very successful but who are socially irresponsible, charming manipulators and chronic liars, for example (the so-called "borderline personality disorder" may be sociopathy in the middle class; see Pope et al. 1983). The problem is that we don't have anything to measure, because we don't understand the underlying chemistry or physiology of the process which makes sociopaths. We do have some pretty interesting clues, however.

There are several theories about what sociopathy "really" is. The oldest, according to Goodwin and Guze (1979), is that sociopathy is moral insanity. These are just people without any moral sense at all, while in all other aspects of intelligence they may be quite normal. Modern versions of this theory are that sociopaths are people without fear or without the ability to feel guilt. (The implication of this is interesting. We have a folk notion that love, affection, and emotional support will make our children into decent people. Not so, according to this idea. Fear is what will make them act right.)

The most interesting idea about the mechanism of sociopathy is found in Mednick and Hutchings (1978). Sociopaths seem to have a very low level of CNS arousal. Once they are aroused it takes a long time for this arousal to dissipate. Their idea is that any of us might be tempted to rob the cash register at the convenience store, for example. The idea makes us anxious, we decide not to, and immediately are rewarded by the dissipation of the fear and anxiety. For the sociopath the fear and anxiety do not dissipate, and he never develops an internal reinforcement system for moral behavior.

With arbitrary and fairly harsh diagnostic criteria which are confounded with social class, the prevalence of sociopathy ranges from two to ten per cent of the male population. The low figure is characteristic of middle-class and upper-class neighborhoods, while the higher prevalence is characteristic of lower-class inner city populations. Sociopathy probably predisposes to downward social mobility.

The same genes in females cause them to exhibit Briquet's syndrome or hysteria. This is a pattern of multiple medical complaints in the absence of any objective sign of disease. These females typically have a large number of aches, pains, menstrual disorders, anxieties, fatigue, dizziness, and the like. In one study they had approximately three times the number of major operations per 100 person-years as did even sick control subjects (Goodwin and Guze 1979). Their general presentation of self is as a helpless person who needs input from a male. A psychiatrist friend tells us that there is a temporary "cure" when these patients are reassigned to female physicians: they apparently are not interested in telling their story to other females.

Hysterics also have many of the same traits in their histories as do sociopaths, such as juvenile delinquency, chronic lying, fighting, and especially sexual promiscuity and illegitimate offspring. There is an excellent fit of family data to a model in which the threshold for sociopathy in a female is higher than in a male. There are some full-blown female sociopaths; according to this model they have a much greater dose of the pertinent genes than does the average male sociopath. The prediction is that sociopathy in relatives of female sociopaths will be much more frequent than in relatives of males. This is borne out very clearly by the data. See Figure 3 (from Cloninger et al. 1978).

Figure 3

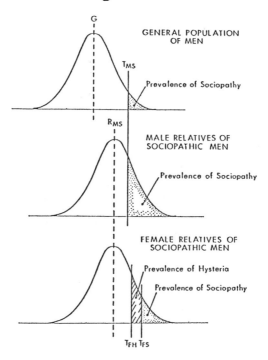

Hypothetical underlying liability to hysteria or sociopathy, showing the two thresholds in females. From Cloninger, Reich, and Guze 1978.

There are probably environmental factors that influence the expression of these conditions, but no one knows what they are. It is clear that there is a strong genetic component to these disorders. It would probably appear much stronger if the diagnostic criteria were not so arbitrary. Robins (1966), in her classic follow-up study of children referred to a guidance clinic in the 1920s, comments that the sibs of sociopaths had almost as much disorder in their lives as did the probands in the study.

The clearest evidence is from the studies in Denmark of children of sociopathic criminals who were raised by foster parents. In these studies there is a clear elevation of sociopathy in the biological relatives of sociopathic probands but no elevated sociopathy rate in the adoptive relatives (Mednick and Christiansen 1977).

Figure 4

A. Psychopathy in relatives

	Biological relatives	Adoptive relatives
Psychopathic adoptees	12/305 = 3.9%	1/131 = 0.8%
Control adoptees	4/285 = 1.4%	2/133 = 1.5%

B. Psychopathy in parents

	Biological parents	Adoptive parents
Psychopathic adoptees	5/111 = 4.5%	1/111 = 0.9%
Control adoptees	1/113 = 0.9%	0/114 = 0%

C. Psychopathy in fathers

	Biological fathers	Adoptive fathers
Psychopathic adoptees	5/54 = 9.3%	1/54 = 1.9%
Control adoptees	1/56 = 1.8%	0/57 = 0%

Sociopathy (=psychopathy) in relatives of sociopathic and control Danish Adoptees. Mednick and Hutchings 1978.

It seems to us that this pair of "disorders" is precisely what a cynical evolutionist would expect to see in a species with the kind of convoluted social ties which we have. The male bearing these genes is beautifully designed to cheat on his social obligations, whether that be by robbing a store or by leaving illegitimate children in his wake. The hysteric shows in exaggerated form the characteristics of a female designed to feign need, extract resources from males, and play the breeder strategy of Table 1.

The adaptive interpretation of sociopathy and hysteria raises some interesting questions. First, if these people are the tail of an underlying normal distribution of something, then what is the other tail? Of course that depends on what the underlying trait "really" is. If it is conscience, then who are the people that have too much as opposed to too little conscience? If that underlying trait is not conscience but fear, are some kinds of neurosis just the other end of the spectrum from sociopaths? Does this account for some of the class differences in both sociopathy and neurosis?

Finally, what kinds of subsistence and social organization would favor or disfavor the sociopathy/hysteria complex? If they are cheaters, then they should enjoy an advantage in large-scale urban societies. In small face-to-face societies they would be found out and would lose their advantage right away. It is difficult to imagine a !Kung Bushman sociopath, for example; non-reciprocators would be quickly identified and publicized in that kind of group. Any situation where economic and social relations can be transient should favor these people. They are good candidates for being a frequency dependent polymorphism, since the fitness of being a sociopath should decrease as there are more of them around. The more frequent they are in the environment, the more aware and cautious the rest of us will be. Meanwhile, they are probably Darwin's answer to the welfare state.

Father Absence and Cultural Transmission

Most of us in anthropology assume that people behave differently from each other because of learning and socialization. As the geneticists realize, most children are raised by their parents, with whom they share genes. Hence many apparent effects of socialization could as well be due to genetic transmission. For example, it is often repeated that child abusers were themselves abused as children. The implication is that being abused did something to them, predisposing them later to abuse the next generation, but genetic transmission is just as compatible with the data.

There are several areas where there is very little doubt that cultural transmission predominates, such as language and other aspects of what we call culture. There are convincing examples of prepared learning, such as the Westermarck effect (see van den Berghe 1982, for a review) and probably language learning. On the other hand the situation with respect to things we call personality or temperament is less clear. Our evolutionist's viewpoint may guide us in sorting these things out.

Designing a flexible intelligent creature to participate in a complex social system is a difficult job, much more difficult than designing an automaton like an insect for the same role. Insects lack our learning abilities, yet they have very satisfactory complex social institutions. Many but not all humans participate in complex institutions, but we have only been doing it for a dozen or so millenia.

What are the costs and benefits of our intelligence? It seems to us that the major problem is the gullibility precipice. We suspect that if we plot intelligence (defined here as the ability to acquire and manipulate information about the world--yes, it is vague) against individual fitness in human evolution the graph might look something like Figure 5.

Figure 5

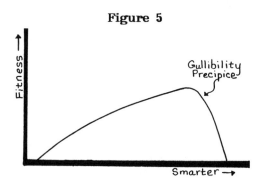

Hypothetical relationship between learning ability (horizontal) and individual fitness (vertical).

The problem is that the better able an individual is to take in and comprehend information, the more vulnerable that individual is to being manipulated by others. Our students, for example, are benefited (presumably) by learning the names of fossil hominids from us. They are not benefited by learning from us that morally correct behavior involves working in our garden. If they were really carelessly designed to learn anything--the conventional idea of intelligence--then presumably we could "teach" them any number of outrages which would benefit our fitness but not theirs. From the viewpoint of an evolutionist humans teeter on the edge of the precipice and often fall in; witness the zeal of participants in warfare. Wilson (1978) contains an interesting discussion of the evolution of religion and ideology. Barkow (1983) summarizes his perspective on intelligence, motivation, and culture. He points out many examples of cultural traits that reduce the fitness of everyone and argues, as we do here, for examination of the learning mechanisms underlying culture.

A second area of compromise in the design of a creature which learns is that between late or contemporary learning and early or prepared learning. The advantage to me of learning, say, my reproductive strategy or style when I am an adult is that I am then least gullible and vulnerable to misdirection. The advantage, on the other hand, to having learned it (that is, having had it set) when I was very young is that I could have practiced it for all those years I was growing up. We know that practice is an important aspect of the very long pre-reproductive part of the lives of mammals, and especially primates. If I don't learn something until adulthood, I probably lose in competition with conspecifics who have practiced it since infancy.

Draper and Harpending (1982) interpret a series of well known correlates of being reared in father absent households in just these terms. They argue that all the consequences of this household structure represent evolved sensitive period learning or "setting" of interests and preferences in the child. These interests and preferences facilitate later reproductive behavior.

Father absence has been an important topic in the fields of education and social welfare, since it is characteristic of very poor people in the United States. Some sociologists (Banfield 1968) even define the lower socioeconomic class in terms of its matrifocal families. John and Beatrice Whiting and numerous collaborators have looked at father absence across cultures and they have found, in general, the same effects as have been found within the United States and other stratified societies (summary in Whiting and Whiting 1975). In other words, there are some reliable consequences of being reared in a matrifocal household regardless of whether or not such a household is the local norm. These consequences are different for males and females.

Father-absent males exhibit lowered spatial abilities on standardized educational tests along with some augmentation of verbal type abilities. They are more likely to be in male gangs and to be involved in crime as they mature, and they characteristically derogate females and things feminine. These effects are not limited to poor people, although they are probably different for different social classes. A sample of father absent Harvard freshmen exhibited the loss of spatial ability and gain in verbal ability seen in other studies, but they showed none of the aggressiveness nor gang behavior described elsewhere. They did differ from controls in their stated intentions for post-graduate work: they planned to travel and "bum around for a while" while controls were much more career oriented. (Carlsmith 1964; Draper and Harpending 1982).

It is immediately apparent that the complex of traits borne by father-absent males is precisely that which a male designed to compete with other males would have. Verbal facility and repartee are two of the most often reported mechanisms by which males engage in face-to-face interpersonal competition. Oratory, bombast, and rhetoric seem to be fairly reliable markers of cultures or social groups within cultures where male-male competition is widespread and pervasive. Further, father-absent males show a predilection for membership in male gangs and local military units where they exist. Whiting and Whiting (1975) suggest that the whole complex of father-absence is an adaptation to warfare. We do not disagree with their insight, except insofar as we suggest that father-absence may may lead to males who are more interested in war and raiding and who are better at it. In this sense it may also be a cause of chronic local warfare and raiding, whether in lower class street gangs or among swiddening villages.

Second, verbal tests probably measure a more general facility with people and with interpersonal interaction and manipulation. A well-designed cad should be skilled at predicting and manipulating the behavior or others. These abilities serve him in avoiding unwelcome confrontations with other males as well as in persuading and coercing females. (Note that it is almost impossible to discuss these issues without using language that is very heavily laden with our values. The benign description of the kinds of abilities we are discussing is "communication skills." If we say that father-absent males are, according to our hypothesis, better at interpersonal interaction, that sounds acceptable, while when we say that they are better at manipulation, that sounds mean. We believe that these two descriptions are entirely synonymous and that this is a good example of the way that language is a hindrance and a trap for social scientists.)

In view of the advantages of early learning as opposed to learning in adulthood, it is interesting that the documented effects of father absence only occur if it occurs very early, preferably before the age of three, in the life of the developing child. Later father absence doesn't work. Whatever the proximate mechanisms leading to this learning of reproductive strategy, they work so early that they are probably not mediated at all by language.

Most of the researchers who have written about father absence have been interested in the topic because of its effects on cognitive skills and hence on educational performance of children from father-absent families. They have always been puzzled because the loss of spatial ability and the gain of verbal ability associated with father absence appear in males but not females. Why doesn't it affect females?

If the early tracking associated with father absence is really learning a reproductive strategy, then we don't expect females to be learning skills which will help them in the dominance struggles of males. We expect that the outcome of females being reared father-absent is to "learn" that males will not provide resources. Such females time reproduction according to resources currently at hand. Unlike father-present females, they do not delay reproduction until they have input from a bonded mate. The data do show that father-absent females exhibit precisely this set of behaviors (Hetherington 1972; Draper and Harpending 1982). They are more oriented to males at a young age, they are more flirtatious, and they start their sex lives earlier. The exceptions in the Hetherington study were daughters of widows, who were extremely sexually conservative and reticent, much more so than the daughters of intact families--behaviors appropriate to females who had learned that males were very important to reproduction and that reproduction must not be initiated until a bonded male was present to provide resources.

Without the insights from thinking about reproductive strategies, it has been difficult to make sense out of the father-absence literature, particularly the cognitive effects. The evolutionary viewpoint does seem to make it all make sense. It is an interesting tale because it is an effect of socialization and learning, but one far different from the boring "children learn what they are taught" kind of socialization. In the father absence model, the learning process is determined by the child, who is designed to sense household structure (in some unknown way--probably an interaction with the mother) and respond to it. The child seems to do this without any regard for what the adults are trying to teach it. Whether or not this model holds up over time, it is useful if it makes us question our deep assumption that adults teach and children learn. Teaching seems to work with neutral material not connected in any immediate way to fitness, like multiplication tables. In other domains active prepared learning by the developing organism may be much more widespread than we like to acknowledge. It is as

if humans are, to some degree, protected from the gullibility precipice by early prepared learning mechanisms. The
American belief that we "shape" our children is perhaps due
for reevaluation.

The Socialization Environment

Above we have raised the issues of ways in which readiness to learn certain things has been shaped by selection.
This prepared learning is presumably set in the genome.
Individuals sense attributes of their post-natal environment
and adapt phenotypically in the appropriate manner. The
apparent childhood sensitivity to household structure
resulting in early tracking for reproductive style is an
example of such flexibility in behavioral development.

An analogous mechanism which may account for apparent
differences in learning outcomes in early childhood is "kin
salience." We know that biological parents will favor their
own offspring; it is also probable that offspring will favor
parents with something that might be described as height-
ened awareness. Infants develop strong bonds with their
primary caretakers. The interpretation that this attachment
drive is built in is strengthened by the many studies of
human and non-humans which show how normal development
is deranged in the individual when the established attachment figure is removed or denied from birth. We do not
know as yet, however, whether high relatedness between
primary caretakers and offspring may configure the
dynamics of interaction in a way that is different from the
configuration of interaction between infants and teacher/
models of lesser or no genetic relatedness. A proposal of
this sort muddies the distinction between heredity and
environment; children are likely to learn differently from
their biological parents as opposed to non-kin.

Studies of childhood socialization have always been
troubled by the fact that their subjects were being reared
by their biological parents. Researchers overwhelmingly
attribute outcome in the children to things which parents do
to or for their children, while they ignore the fact that

natural children share 50 percent of each parent's genes and are rather likely to develop in ways concordant with their parents' expectations, whether latent or manifest. Studies of assortative mating show that additional mechanisms are at work which sort out certain sources of diversity between mates.

An obvious way to test these ideas is with children and adoptive parents, where comparisons can be made between parent/adoptive child dyads and parent/natural child dyads. The population of adoptees and parents would have to be screened extremely carefully, for it is known that both populations differ substantially from a random sample of the general population. For example, adoptive parents are older, more affluent, have more education, more stable marriages, higher I.Q.'s and better overall health than the population means for these attributes. Further, the pool of adoptees is biased in certain directions associated with the factors which have led the biological parents to give them up for adoption in the first place (Horn et al. 1975).

What aspects of parent-child interaction should be watched and at what point(s) in the infant's development can we expect that the parent effect will be the greatest? The period of 18 months to about two years of age is a natural starting point, at least. A child of this age is at an interesting stage for reasons having to do with its own developmental readiness and because this is the age at which children in many societies are turned over to non-parental caretakers. From about 18 months of age the care and management of children is conducted through increasingly distal means. Earlier in life children require physical handling for transport, feeding, and toileting, while the older child is advanced in neuromotor terms. It can get about on its own, initiate separation from the parent who increasingly must resort to language to control the child and to increased vigilance to keep track of the child's whereabouts. Similarly, the more independent offspring must have ways of monitoring the parent, her whereabouts, her approval or disapproval, and the like. Therefore toddlerhood should be a period during which infants are especially cognizant of parents and sensitive to their cues.

Attachment theory, of course, incorporates the notion that the attachment behaviors in toddlers have been selected because they promote the survival of an infant in a species such as ours where the young mature slowly and remain dependent on intensive care from the mother for many years.

Our suggestion here is that during the toddler period the infant is maximally disposed to couple its own modus vivendi with that of the parent. However, this is precisely the point at which parents in certain kinds of societies deflect the child's attempts to gain their nearness and attention onto other caregivers. In terms of our previous discussion, this is the age of abandonment. Children clearly can survive under a variety of caretaking regimes. We intend no Western presumption that our middle-class pattern is superior. We do suggest, however, that being socialized in the post-eighteen month period by biological parents can have different outcomes for what is learned and how it is learned, especially in contrast to the alternate condition in which children are socialized in toddler-hood by various others, often a multi-aged peer group. The phenomena associated with father-absence that we discussed above may be only part of a variety of developmental possibilities sensitive to change at this time.

There are many implications for education and the organization of social groups that result from this type of interpretation. While the tended child of a nuclear family is interacting with older, knowledgeable parents who are genetically related adults, the village child is interacting with relatively ignorant children of much less genetic relatedness. The latter kind of child garners resources in proportion to his ability to manipulate social relations within his peer group, so that social skills are very important for survival. Further, the peer group is the major resource that such a child can access. The nuclear family child, on the other hand, has only a few significant others to deal with and, on the average, they are a lot older and more skilled. There is little payoff to social manipulation for him. Freed of much of the burden of interpersonal manipulation, he can use his brain for other kinds of learning.

Conclusions

Anthropology is fascinating for many reasons, a major reason being that there are so many approaches to understanding the diversity of human behavior. Our colleagues are arranged on both sides of the fence separating the sciences and the humanities. The strength of anthropology is that we embrace these diverse approaches without trying to accomodate them all into a formless mush. In this paper we have tried to follow some of the logical implications of an evolutionist's approach to human culture.

Our first principal conclusion was that language is a complex phenomenon and that this complexity has implications for social science that are not well understood in the literature. There is no good reason to expect that humans naively communicate truth when they talk. Whether or not deceit and manipulation are conscious or not, we should expect to find widespread manipulation and falsehood in human cultures as well as truth and shared meaning. The notion that culture is an adaptation, that it benefits groups, and that it is somehow greater than the individual, needs to be very carefully reevaluated. As an example we used the complex of fear and denigration of women characteristic of many middle-range societies around the world. This complex makes little sense according to most functionalist interpretations of culture, while if it is viewed as the reticulation of males trying to manipulate each other (consciously or not: we can't know), then it makes logical sense.

Our second point was that we should try to divorce our feelings from our scientific inference. This is easy to do in the hard sciences, it gets difficult the more "relevant" the science becomes (for example, ecology in the early seventies), and it is very hard for social scientists. We presented a simple model of optimal maternal investment in children as a function of age which predicted relative abandonment soon after weaning. In many groups children of this age and older are turned loose from the mother and left to forage with other children. Mothers terminate most of their investment rather abruptly in these groups, and the pattern recalls that of other primates. In this country we would call this child neglect, and our personal feelings make it difficult to understand that this is probably a facultative adaptation to certain conditions of food availability and certain maternal fertility strategies.

We then pointed out that we cannot continue to presume that the diversity of human behavior is all culturally transmitted. We discussed the related psychiatric disorders of sociopathy and Briquet's syndrome as genetically transmitted reproductive strategies. We do not have any theory which informs us that these trait complexes should be transmitted genetically, and indeed we were very surprised that the literature reveals little or no cultural transmission of them. Humans, more than any other species, have complex culturally transmitted rule structures. A disinterested evolutionary biologist would predict that cheaters would evolve in the face of such a complex system of reciprocity. A sociopath is simply a cheater, while a female with Briquet's syndrome is a mild sociopath with special adaptations to coax resources from males.

Finally, we discussed the social psychology of father-absence as an example of culturally transmitted strategy differences among us. Children seem to learn a number of things during development that are not taught them, and the consequences of father-absent rearing seem to be of this nature. We presented some arguments about why this learning of reproductive behaviors in early childhood makes sense in a species such as ours where learning during development is critically important for adult fitness and where there is a great variety of reproductive arrangements across cultures and over time. The father-absent phenomena may be part of a more general developmental choice of whether to invest learning effort in social or in non-social phenomena. Children raised in the context of a nurturant nuclear family can and probably do invest more in learning non-social and impersonal aspects of the world, while in the context of relative abandonment after weaning social skills are much more vital to the child.

H. Harpending and P. Draper

REFERENCES

Banfield, E.C.
1968   *The Unheavenly City.*   Boston: Little Brown.

Barkow, J.
1983   Why Sociobiology needs the Psychologist:
         Research Strategies in Sociobiology and
         Anthropology. Paper given at the XIth ICAES,
         August, 1983.

Birdsell, J. B.
1968   Some Predictions for the Pleistocene Based on
         Equilibrium Systems Among Recent Hunter-
         Gatherers. In *Man the Hunter,* ed. by R. Lee
         and I. DeVore. Chicago: Aldine, pp. 229-239.

Bohman, M.
1978   Some Genetic Aspects of Alcoholism and
         Criminality. *Archives of General Psychiatry*
         35:269-276.

Brown, G.W.
1979   Learning Disabilities: A Pediatrician's Overview.
         In *The Learning-Disabled Child.* ed. by
         M. Gottlieb, P. Zinkus, and L. Bradford.
         New York: Grune and Strattonpp, pp. 13-45.

Carlsmith, L.
1964   Effect of Early Father Absence on Scholastic
         Aptitude. *Harvard Education Review*   34:3-21.

Cloninger, C.R.
1978   The Antisocial Personality. *Hospital Practice:*
         August:97-106.

Cloninger, C.R., T. Reich, and S.B. Guze
1975a   The Multifactorial Model of Disease Transmission:
           II. Sex Difference in the Familial Transmission
           of Sociopathy. *British Journal of Psychiatry*
           127:11.

1975b   The Multifactorial Model of Disease Transmission:
           III. Familial Relationship between Sociopathy and
           Hysteria. *British Journal of Psychiatry* 127:23-32.

1978   Genetic-environmental Interactions and Anti-
           social Behaviour. In Hare and Shallings, 1978
           (qv),pp. 225-238.

Daly, M. and M. Wilson
1983   *Sex, Evolution, and Behavior.* Second edition.
           Boston: Willard Grant Press.

Dawkins, R.
1976   *The Selfish Gene.* London: Oxford University
           Press.

Draper, P. and H. Harpending
1982   Father Absence and Reproductive Strategy: An
           Evolutionary Perspective. *Journal of Anthropo-
           logical Research.* 38:255-273.

DuBois, C.
1944   *The People of Alor.* Minneapolis: University of
           Minnesota Press.

Feierman, J.
1982   Nocturnalism: An Ethological Theory of Schizo-
           phrenia. *Medical Hypotheses* 9:455-479.

nd   The Manic-Depressive Phenomena I: Hibernation
           as a Biological Research Model. Ms, Vista
           Sandia Hospital, Albuquerque, New Mexico.

H. Harpending and P. Draper

Goodwin, D.W. and S.B. Guze
1979   *Psychiatric Diagnosis.* Second edition. New
        York: Oxford University Press.

Gordon, J.W., and F. Ruddle
1981   Mammalian Gonadal Determination and Gameto-
        genesis. *Science* 211:1265-1271.

Guze, S.B., D.W. Goodwin, and J.B. Crane
1969   Criminality and Psychiatric Disorders. *Archives
        of General Psychiatry* 20:583-591.

Hare, R.D. and D. Schalling, eds.
1978   *Psychopathic Behavior: Approaches to Re-
        search.* New York: John Wiley.

Hetherington, E.M.
1972   Effects of Father Absence on Personality De-
        velopment in Adolescent Daughters. *Developmental
        Psychology* 7:313-326.

Horn, J., M. Green, R. Carney, and M. Erickson
1975   Bias Against Genetic Hypotheses in Adoption
        Studies. *Archives of General Psychiatry*
        32:1365-1367.

Johnson, A.
1978   *Quantification in Cultural Anthropology. An
        Introduction to Research Design.* Stanford:
        Stanford University Press.

Kelekna, P.
1981   Sex Asymmetry in Jivaroan Achuara Society:
        A Cultural Mechanism Promoting Belligerence.
        Dissertation: Albuquerque, University of New
        Mexico.

Korbin, J.E., ed.
1981   *Child Abuse and Neglect: Cross-Cultural
        Perspectives.* Berkeley: University of California
        Press.

LeVine, S. and R. LeVine
1981   Child Abuse and Neglect in Sub-Saharan Africa.
        In Korbin, ed., 1981 (qv), pp. 35-55.

Lewontin, R.
1974   *The Genetic Basis of Evolutionary Change.*
        New York: Columbia University Press.

Maynard Smith, J.
1977   Parental Investment: A Prospective Analysis.
        Animal Behavior 25: 1-9.

1982   *Evolution and the Theory of Games.* Cambridge:
        Cambridge University Press.

Mednick, S. and K.O. Christiansen, eds.
1977   *Biosocial Bases of Criminal Behavior.* New York:
        Gardner.

Mednick, S.A. and B. Hutchings
1978   Genetic and Psychophysiological Factors in
        Asocial Behavior. In Hare and Shallings, 1978
        (qv)., pp. 239-253.

Meggitt, M.
1964   Male Female Relationships in the Highlands of
        New Guinea. *American Anthropologist* 66:204-224.

Mendelson, W., N. Johnson, and M.A. Stewart
1971   Hyperactive Children as Teenagers: a Follow-up
        Study. *Journal of Nervous Mental Disorders.*
        153:273-279.

Murphy, Y. and R. Murphy
1974   *Women of the Forest.* New York: Columbia
        University Press.

Pope, H.G., J.M. Jonas, J.I. Hudson, B.M. Cohen,
    and J.G. Gunderson
1983   The Validity of DSM-III Borderline Personality
        Disorder. *Archives of General Psychiatry* 40:23-30.

Preston, S.H., N. Keyfitz, and R. Schoen
1972   *Causes of Death. Life Tables for National Populations.* New York: Seminar Press.

Robins, L.N.
1971   *Deviant Children Grown Up.* Baltimore: Williams & Wilkins.

1978   Aetiological Implications in Studies of Childhood Histories Relating to Antisocial Personality. In Hare and Schalling, 1978 (qv), pp. 255-272.

Robins, L. and P. O'Neal
1958   Mortality, Mobility, and Crime: Problem Children Thirty Years Later. *American Sociological Review* 23:162-171.

Satterfield, J.H.
1978   The Hyperactive Child Syndrome: a Precursor of Adult Psychopathy. In Hare and Schalling 1978 (qv), pp. 329-346.

Shostak, M.
1976   A !Kung Woman's Memories of Childhood. In *Kalahari Hunter-Gatherers,* ed. by R. Lee and I. DeVore. Cambridge: Harvard University Press.

Trivers, R.
1972   Parental Investment and Sexual Selection. In *Sexual Selection and the Descent of Man, 1871-1971,* ed. by B. Campbell, pp. 136-179 Chicago: Aldine.

van den Berghe, P.L.
1982   Human Inbreeding Avoidance: Culture in Nature. *Behavioral and Brain Sciences* 6:91-123.

Wender P.H. and D.F. Klein
1981   *Mind, Mood and Medicine. A Guide to the New Biopsychiatry.* New York: Farrar, Straus, Giroux.

Whiting, J.W.M. and B.B. Whiting
   1975   Aloofness and Intimacy of Husbands and Wives:
           A Cross Cultural Study. *Ethos* 3:183-207.

Wilson, E.O.
   1978   *On Human Nature.* Cambridge: Harvard University
           Press.

IS HUMAN EVOLUTION PUNCTUATIONAL?

Steven M. Stanley

The punctuational model of evolution can be defined as the proposition that most evolutionary change in the history of life is associated with geologically brief episodes of speciation (phylogenetic branching), whereas phyletic change (transformation of established species) plays a subordinate role. Darwin asserted the alternative, -gradualistic view, which holds that phyletic evolution is the dominant mode of change, and this view prevailed during the first three decades of the Modern Synthesis of evolution. On a smaller scale, the gradualistic view has also dominated the study of human origins, being expressed within numerous textbooks in graphs of human phylogeny that depict a single lineage divided into non-overlapping chronospecies typically labeled *Australopithecus africanus, Homo habilis, Homo erectus,* and *Homo sapiens.*
Implicit here is the Single Species Hypothesis. Based in part on the Gaussian proposition that two sympatric species cannot share the same niche, the Single Species Hypothesis asserts that niches within the Hominidae are so broad that two species of the family could never co-exist for more than a brief interval; through competitive exclusion, one of two sympatric species would quickly eliminate the other. In allowing species to co-occur briefly, the Single Species Hypothesis is compatible with the punctuational model of evolution because the possibility remains that one species might branch rapidly from another and then competitatively

eliminate this parent species. Nonetheless, the Single
Species Hypothesis has usually been associated with the
gradualistic notion that modern humans stand at the top of
a single evolutionary lineage that issued from a gracile
australopithecine stock. The discovery of skulls of *Homo
erectus* and a robust australopithecine at a single collecting
site in East Turkana sediments about 1.6 m.y.-old (Leakey
and Walker, 1976) debunked the Single Species Hypothesis
as a universal tenet for the Hominidae, but this discovery
left open the possibility that the hypothesis might still hold
for the genus *Homo*.

It seems reasonable to apply the label "Single Lineage
Hypothesis" to the more restrictive idea that a single evolutionary lineage arbitrarily divided into the chronospecies
Homo habilis, *Homo erectus*, and *Homo sapiens* includes the
entire evolutionary history of the genus *Homo*. This gradualistic model can be contrasted with the punctuational model
that envisions at least brief overlaps between relatively
stable species that are connected by rapid speciation
events. If the overlaps are brief because of competitive
exclusion, this punctuational model entails a modified
version of the Single Species Hypothesis.

Arguing against the Single Lineage Hypothesis and, in
fact, against a gradualistic pattern for human evolution in
general, is evidence that continues to accumulate indicating
that species of the human family survived for long spans of
time-often in the order of a million years-without undergoing substantial evolutionary change. The stability of species
of animals and plants in general is the kind of evidence
that has led me to adopt the punctuational model of
evolution and to explore its macroevolutionary implications
(Stanley 1979). Accordingly, in the section that follows, I
will summarize evidence for the stability of species in
diverse higher taxa.

The Longevity of Species

Since the modern punctuational model was proposed by Eldredge (1971) and Eldredge and Gould (1972), I have tested it by analyzing the geological longevities of species within higher taxa (Stanley 1975, 1979, 1982). Such analysis is meaningful only when placed in perspective, and this perspective seems best established by application of what I have called the "test of adaptive radiation" (Stanley 1975, 1979). This test compares the geological longevities of fossil species with the lengths of intervals during which large-scale evolutionary changes take place. The fact that these changes are frequently associated with adaptive radiation accounts for the name of the test. If, during a brief geological interval, phyletic evolution (or anagenesis-transformation of an entire lineage), has yielded a major evolutionary change, such as is embodied in the origin of a new genus or family, then the lineage encompassing this change will necessarily be divided into chronospecies of very short duration. On the other hand, persistence of the lineage with little change will produce chronospecies of great duration and will not rapidly yield a new higher taxon. The early Cenozoic adaptive radiation of the mammals illustrates this test.

Particularly revealing are the mammal-bearing strata of the Lower Eocene sequence of the Big Horn Basin. These strata represent an important interval of the mammalian adaptive radiation--an interval during which hundreds of new genera appeared in the world, and perhaps more than twenty new families. Because of their unique richness, the faunas of the Big Horn Basin afford a special opportunity for examining what happened to species during this interval. Here, large numbers of evolutionary lineages have been traced upward through hundreds of meters of sediment by samples collected at intervals of 10 meters--intervals representing perhaps 40,000 to 70,000 years. Large volumes of data gathered by Schankler (1980) supplemented by data gathered by Bakker (see Stanley 1982), reveal that approximately 50 species of mammals survived for intervals

in the order of 2 million years without evolving enough to
be regarded as a new chronospecies. Dentition represents
most of the fossil data here, and not a single species
exhibits appreciable change in diagnostic dental features--
not enough to qualify for a specific name change, to say
nothing of a generic one. The set of fifty or so lineages
that underwent little evolutionary change during two-million
year intervals represents a large sample of the Late Eocene
lineages of North America, and it offers strong evidence
that even during the Early Cenozoic adaptive radiation of
mammals, when numerous higher taxa were originating,
species were remarkably stable entities. Thus, it seems
necessary to invoke punctuational evolutionary steps to
explain the Late Eocene origins of many higher taxa.

Even greater mean longevities are apparent for non-
mammalian taxa (Stanley 1975, 1979, 1982). For higher
plants, seeds are typically diagnostic of species identity,
and about 50% of all species of European higher plants
known from seeds in deposits 4 million years old are alive
today (Leopold 1967). Stebbins (1982) estimates a modal
antiquity greater than 15 million years for woody plant
species of western United States. At a simpler level of
morphology, well-preserved bryophyte floras ranging back
20 million years consist almost entirely of living species
(Dickson 1973).

For non-mammalian terrestrial mammals, species are also
remarkably stable. Of nineteen species of North American
snakes known from the Blancan Stage, which represents the
interval from 4 to 1.5 million years, fourteen species are
alive today (Holman 1981). For beetles, genitalia are
diagnostic of species identity in the Recent and they also
happen to be resistant to decay when buried in the absence
of free oxygen. As it turns out, all known Pleistocene
beetle genitalia are assigned to living species (Coope 1979).
This fact reveals that mean species duration for beetles
exceeds 1 or 2 million years.

For numerous marine taxa, ranging from Foraminifera
and diatoms to bivalves and gastropods, mean species duration is even greater, approaching or exceeding 10 m.y.
(Stanley 1979, 1982).

Thus, abundant data have led me to generalize that, barring extinction, a typical established species, whether a species of mammals, land plants, insects, or marine invertebrates, will undergo little measurable morphological change during an interval that represents in the order of one hundred thousand or a million generations (Stanley 1982).

The Stability of Hominid Species

One might argue that the punctuational pattern evident in the phylogenies of numerous non-human taxa can be extrapolated to human evolution. Given our uncertainty about what causes evolutionary stability of species and given the novel behavioral ecology of human species, however, such a deductive approach would be hazardous. It should also prove unnecessary, because the quality of the known fossil record of the Hominidae is rapidly reaching the level that will permit direct evaluation of the tempo of human evolution. Indeed, during the past few years, human phylogeny has come to look more and more punctuational. Several important species can be seen to have survived for long stretches of geological time without undergoing substantial transformation.

One cannot establish a gradualistic pattern for human phylogeny simply by plotting mean body weights or cranial capacities for *Australopithecus africanus, Homo habilis, H. erectus,* and *H. sapiens* for single points in time and finding crude alignment (Cronin et al. 1981). Much finer temporal resolution is needed for discernment of an evolutionary pattern. Evolutionary stasis of individual species and overlap between species are the kinds of evidence that can refute a gradualistic hypothesis. Both conditions are now evident in important segments of hominid phylogeny, and I will review these briefly, hoping to stimulate specialists to delve further into the issue.

Australopithecus afarensis.   Recent revision of ages of the Hadar fossils assigned to *Australopithecus afarensis* places some at 3 m.y., or slightly younger (Brown 1982; Boaz et al. 1982). Inasmuch as the specimens from Laetoli

assigned to *A. afarensis* approach 3.8 m.y. in age (Leakey
et al. 1976), this species (or a narrow clade that includes
it) can now be seen to have survived, more or less unchanged, for nearly a million years. This large interval of
approximate stasis is recognized from the evidence of just
two collecting sites and can only be expected to grow still
longer with future discoveries. Splitting off some individuals of the Hadar "population" as one or more separate
species (Olson 1981) would not remove the evidence for
stasis, and synonymizing *A. afarensis* with the poorly dated
species *A. africanus,* as favored by some workers (Tobias
1981) could only alter the species' range in the direction of
greater longevity. Also not to be ignored here is evidence
that gracile australopithecines may have survived in the
East Turkana region until about 1.5 million years ago
(specimens KNM-ER 1805 and 1813), long after they had
first existed in the south and even after *Homo erectus* was
in existence (Leakey and Walker 1980).

Australopithecus robustus/boisei.   The robust australopithecines, whether forming one species or two or more,
represent a segment of phylogeny that encompasses little
evolutionary change (how else could some experts consider
them to form a single species?). The robust australopithecines survived, with little apparent change, for at
least a million years, from about 2 million years ago to
about 1 million years ago (see, for example, Pilbeam 1975;
Howell 1978). Thus, the segment of phylogeny that they
represent, though a side issue in the evolutionary sequence
leading to modern humans, illustrates evolutionary stability
within hominid evolution.

Homo erectus.   Morphological stability in the history of
Homo erectus is especially striking because the younger
populations of this species were not far removed in time
from the earliest modern humans. Plotting cranial capacity,
biauricular breadth, width of the M molar, and robusticity
index for *Homo erectus* against time, Rightmire (1981) found
no statistically significant trends. It is true that the small
samples of measurements available for such analysis make it
inevitable that slopes of regression lines cannot be shown to
differ from zero with a high degree of certainty (Levinton

1982). This, however, is not the appropriate question. No lineage could be expected to exhibit perfect stasis (no net evolutionary change whatever in any measurable parameter). The question is whether the data indicate that phyletic trends within *Homo erectus*, if projected forward in time, would have been strong enought to yield modern humans. According to Rightmire's data, the trend most likely for *Homo erectus* is in cranial capacity. It seems apparent, however, that not even here could a possible trend, if projected slightly forward from 300,000 or 200,000 years ago to 100,000 or 40,000 years ago, yield the mean brain capacity of *Homo sapiens*, to say nothing of the mean brain capacity of Neanderthal (more than 1400 cc). Some form of acceleration of evolution is required.

The temporal continuity of the Acheulian culture, which like *Homo erectus* fossils appeared more or less at the start of the Pleistocene, represents another aspect of evolutionary conservatism in this species, and can now be see to have extended east of India (Okladinikov 1978).

Postcranial data provide still another kind of evidence for stasis. With strong statistical evidence, Kennedy (1983) has recently shown that the femur of *Homo erectus:* 1) is morphologically distinct from the femurs of *H. sapiens* and *Australopithecus* and 2) exhibits extremely little change over a span of at least 1.5 m.y. An interesting aspect of this analysis is that specimen KNM ER 1481a, a virtually complete femur from Lake Turkana dated at about 2 m.y., is so similar as to appear conspecific with *Homo erectus* femurs, including two from Choukoutien less than 0.5 m.y. old.

Neanderthal and *Homo sapiens sapiens.* Classical European Neanderthal populations may have their phyletic ancestry in populations more than 250,000 years old, represented by the Steinheim and Swanscombe crania (Santa Luca 1978; Stringer 1981), but it is evident that Neanderthals underwent little morphological change between about 100,000 and 35,000 or 30,000 years ago. This latter interval is by no means great in comparison to mean species duration for the Mammalia in general. Nevertheless, in representing more than 3,000 generations, it is substantial in population genetic terms.

As an outsider to paleoanthropology, I must express surprise at the prevailing opinion among paleoanthropologists that Neanderthal was a subspecies of *Homo sapiens* rather than a discrete species. The distinctive features of Neanderthal are well known--the long low-vaulted skull; the heavy brow ridges; the gap posterior to the molars; the prognathous jaw; the massive limb bones; and the characteristic features of the pelvis, scapula, and hands and feet. The morphological differences between Neanderthals and modern humans are far greater than those separating many other pairs of mammal species. In fact, the low-vaulted skull, massive brow ridges, and prognathous jaw of Neanderthal establish a strong resemblance of *Homo erectus*. The general impression of similarity here (Stanley 1981:152-153) receives quantitative support in a comparison of cranial outlines, which shows Neanderthal to be closer in form to *Homo erectus* than to modern humans (Walker in press).

It has perhaps been difficult for many paleoanthropologists to accept the possibility that there has existed on earth a big brained, culturally advanced species other than *Homo sapiens.* Certainly a prevalence of gradualistic thinking has been another factor contributing to the idea that Neanderthal was a subspecies of *Homo sapiens*. The idea that Neanderthal might have been transformed gradually into modern *Homo sapiens* is still widely entertained (Brace 1979; Wolpoff 1980; Smith 1982). *Wholesale* phyletic transformation of Neanderthal to modern *Homo sapiens* in Europe is ruled out, however, by the discovery of a partially articulated "classical" Neanderthal skeleton of Upper Paleolithic age (between 35,000 and 30,000 years) at Saint-Cesaire, France (Leveque and Vandermeersch 1981). Thus, Neanderthal survived in Europe after anatomically modern humans were present. I agree with Stringer (1982) on the importance of this fact with regard to the occurrence of the Skhul and Qafzeh hominids of the modern type in Near Eastern deposits almost certainly more than 40,000 years old. The suggestion is that modern humans replaced Neanderthal by northward migration.

In addition, femurs of essentially modern form have been found in deposits of eastern and southern Africa older than

0.1 m.y. This suggests that the characteristic femoral morphology of European Neanderthal represents a derived state with regard to that of modern humans (Kennedy, in press). However and wherever humans of the modern type("*Homo sapiens sapiens*") originated, it is also evident that they experienced remarkable evolutionary stability in Europe for more than 30,000 years, or on the order of 10 generations.

Discussion

Certain net trends are evident in human evolution, among them increase in brain size and body weight. A simple plot including an estimated mean value of brain size or body weight for each of four species at one time in its history (Cronin et al. 1981) is not, however, sufficient to establish a gradualistic trend. This "connect-the-dots" approach lumps temporal data that might show relative stasis for each species. In ignoring many other morphological features, it also fails to take into account the fact that certain morphological parameters did not exhibit even net trends but instead underwent evolutionary reversals. This is certainly true of robusticity, which increased in the transition from gracile australopithecines to *Homo erectus* and then decreased again in the transition from *Homo erectus* (or a species descended from it) to modern *Homo sapiens.*

ACKNOWLEDGEMENTS

I thank the Anthropology Department of the University of California, Los Angeles, for giving me the opportunity to participate in the Harry Hoijer Lecture Series, and I thank Gail E. Kennedy, in particular, for her useful suggestions for the improvement of my manuscript.

86   S. Stanley

REFERENCES

Boaz, N.T., F.C. Howell, and M.L. McCrossin
   1982   Faunal age of the Usno, Shungura B and Hadar
           Formations, Ethiopia. *Nature* 300:633-635.

Brace, C.L.
   1969   Krapina "classic" Neanderthals and the evolution
           of the European face. *Journal of Human Evolu-
           tion* 8:527-550.

Brown, F.H.
   1982   Tulu Bor Tuff at Koobi Fora correlated with the
           Sidi Hakoma Tuff at Hadar. *Nature* 300:631-633.

Coope, G.R.
   1970   Interpretations of Quaternary insect fossils.
           Annual Review of Entomology 15:97-120.

Cronin, J.E., N.T. Boaz, C.B. Stringer, and Y. Rak
   1981   Tempo and mode in hominid evolution. *Nature*
           292:113-122.

Dickson, J.H.
   1973   *Bryophytes of the Pleistocene: The British
           Record and its Chorological and Ecological
           Implications.* Cambridge: Cambridge University
           Press.

Eldredge, N.
   1971   The allopatric model and phylogeny in Paleozoic
           invertebrates. *Evolution* 25:156-167.

Eldredge, N. and S.J. Gould
   1972   Punctuated equilibria: an alternative to phyletic
           gradualism. In *Models in Paleobiology,* ed. by
           T.J.M. Schopf. San Francisco: Freeman,
           Cooper, and Co., pp. 82-115.

Holman, J.A.
1981   A review of North American Pleistocene snakes.
        Publication of the Museum, Michigan State
        University Paleontology Series   1:261-306.

Howell, F.C.
1981   Homindae. In *Evolution of African Mammals*, ed.
        by V.J. Maglio and H.B.S. Cooke. Cambriage:
        Harvard University Press, pp. 154-248.

Kennedy, G.E.
1983   A morphometric and taxonomic assessment of a
        hominine femur from the Lower Member, Koobi
        Fora, Lake Turkana. *American Journal of*
        Physical Anthropology   61:429-436.

1984   The emergence of *Homo Sapiens*: the post-
        cranial evidence. *Man* 19:94-110.

Leakey, M.D., R.L. Hay, G.H. Curtis, R.E. Drake,
M.K. Jackes, and T.D. White
1976   Fossil hominids from the Laetolil Beds.
        Nature 262:460-466.

Leakey, R.E.F. and A.C. Walker
1976   *Australopithecus*, *Homo erectus*, and the single
        species hypothesis. *Nature* 261:572-574.

1980   On the status of   *Australopithecus afarensis*.
        Science 207:1102-1103.

Leopold, E.B.
1967   Late Cenozoic patterns of plant extinction. In
        Pleistocene Extinction: The Search for a Cause,
        ed. by P.S. Martin and H.E. Wright. New
        Haven: Yale University Press, pp. 203-246.

Leveque, F. and B. Vandermeersch
1981   Le Neandertalien de Saint-Cesaire. *La*
        Recherche 12:241-244.

Levinton, J.S.
1982   Evolutionary stasis in *Homo erectus*?
        Paleobiology 8:307.

Okladinikov, A.P.
1978   The Paleolithic of Mongolia. In *Early Paleolithic
        in South and East Asia*, ed. by F. Ikawa-Smith.
        The Hague: Mouton Publishers pp. 317-325.

Olson, T.R.
1981   Basicranial morphology of the extant hominoids and
        Pliocene hominids: The new material from the
        Hadar Formation, Ethiopia, and its significance in
        early human evolution and taxonomy. In *Aspects of
        Human Evolution*, ed. by C.B. Stringer. London:
        Taylor and Francis, pp. 99-128.

Pilbeam, D.R.
1975   Middle Pleistocene hominids. In *After the
        Australopithecines*, ed. by K.W. Butzer and
        G.L. Issac. The Hague: Mouton Publishers,
        pp. 809-856.

Rightmire, G.P.
1981   Patterns of evolution in *Homo erectus.*
        Paleobiology 7:241-246.

Santa Luca, A.P.
1978   A re-examination of presumed Neanderthal-like
        fossils. *Journal of Human Evolution* 7:619-636.

Schankler, D.
1980   Faunal zonation of the Willwood Formation in the
        Central Bighorn Basin, Wyoming. *University of
        Michigan Papers in Paleontology* 24:99-114.

Smith, F.H.
1982   Upper Pleistocene hominid evolution in south-
        central Europe: A review of the evidence and
        analysis of trends. *Current Anthropology*
        23:667-703.

Stanley, S.M.
1975   A theory of evolution above the species level.
          Proceedings of the National Academy of Science,
          USA 72:646-650.

1979   *Macroevolution: Pattern and Process.* San
          Francisco: Freeman.

1981   *The New Evolutionary Timetable: Fossils,*
          Genes, and the Origin of Species. New York:
          Basic Books.

1982   Macroevolution and the fossil record. *Evolution*
          36:460-473.

Stebbins, G.L.
1982   Perspectives in evolutionary theory. *Evolution*
          36:1109-1118.

Stringer, C.B.
1981   The dating of European middle Pleistocene
          hominids and the existence of *Homo erectus* in
          Europe. *Anthropologie* 19:1-14.

1982   Comment. *Current Anthropology* 23:690-691.

Tobias, P.V.
1981   " *Australopithecus afarensis* " and *A. africanus*;
          critique and an alternative hypothesis.
          Palaeotologica Africana 23:1-7.

Walker, A.
nd   Extinction in hominid evolution. In *Extinctions,*
          ed. by M.H. Nitecki. In press. Chicago:
          University of Chicago Press.

Wolpoff, M.H.
1980   *Paleoanthropology.* New York: Knopf.

OUR CONTRIBUTORS

LUIGI L. CAVALLI-SFORZA is professor of Genetics, Stanford University. He receive his M.D. from the University of Pavia in 1944. He has worked in bacterial genetics, the in human population genetics. Since 1966 he has carried out field work on Africa Pygmies, which still continues, and has recently developed an interest in cultur transmission and evolution. Recent publications include *Cultural Transmission ar Evolution: A Quantitative Approach* (with M. Feldman 1981); and *The Neolithic Transitic and the Genetics of Populations in Europe* (with A. Ammerman 1984). He is the editor of book on African Pygmies to appear soon.

PATRICIA DRAPER is associate professor, Department of Individual and Family Studies College of Human Development, Pennsylvania State University. She received her Ph.D. i Anthropology from Harvard University in 1972. She has conducted field research i Botswana and Namibia among !Kung Bushmen. Her research interests include cross cultural child development, biological and cultural bases of human sex roles, an ethology. Her publications include "The Learning Environment for Aggression and Ant. Social Behavior among the !Kung" (1978);"Father Absence: An Evolutionary Perspective (1983); and "Parent Investment and the Child's Environment" (1985).

HENRY HARPENDING is professor of Anthropology at Pennsylvania State University. H received his Ph.D. from Harvard University in 1972. He has carried out field work amon the !Kung Bushmen and has published extensively on the population structure an population genetics of southern African populations. His research interests also includ the development of models in population genetics and in the evolution of social behavior Recent publications include "Population Structure of Ghanzi and Ngamiland. !Kung" (wit LuAnn Wandsnider 1982); "Chemical Systematics and Human Populations" (with R. War 1982); and "Primate Population Structure: Evaluation of Field Data" (with S. Cowan 1985)

STEVEN M. STANLEY is professor of Paleobiology at The Johns Hopkins University. H received his Ph.D. from Yale University in 1968. His research has dealt with th functional morphology of fossil organisms and on rates, trends, and patterns of evolution His recent work has focused on the punctuational model of evolution and on mas extinctions. Among his publications are "A Theory of Evolution above the Species Level (1975); "Clades versus Clones in Evolution: Why We Have Sex" (1975); *Macroevolution Pattern and Process* (1979); *The New Evolutionary Timetable; Fossils, Genes, and th Origin of Species* (1981); and *Earth and Life Through Time* (1985).

THE EDITOR

B.J. WILLIAMS is professor of Anthropology at the University of California, Los Angeles. He received a Ph.D. in Anthropology and Human Genetics from the University of Michiga in 1965. His research interests include the breeding structure of human populations an behavioral genetics and evolution. Among his publications are *A Model of Band Societ: (1974); Evolution and Human Origins* (1979); "A Critical Review of Models in Sociobiology (1980); and "A Covariance Structure Model for Quantitative Genetic Research" (with S Smalley and others 1985).